D0498590

THE DIALECT POETRY

OF CLAUDE McKAY

Two Volumes in One

PREFACE BY

WAYNE COOPER

AYER COMPANY PUBLISHERS, INC.
NORTH STRATFORD, NH 03590

Reprint Edition, 2003
Ayer Company Publishers, Inc.
Ayer Road
North Stratford, NH 03590

Reprint Edition, 1977
Arno Press, Inc.

Reprinted from a copy in
The Library, University of Illinois
At Urbana-Champaign

LC# 73-38014

ISBN 0-8369-8982-1

Manufactured in the United States of America

DIALECT POETRY

CLAUDE M'KAY.

THE DIALECT POETRY OF CLAUDE McKAY

Two Volumes in One

Volume I
SONGS OF JAMAICA

Volume II
CONSTAB BALLADS

**With a Preface to this edition by
Wayne Cooper**

The Black Heritage Library Collection

BOOKS FOR LIBRARIES PRESS
PLAINVIEW, NEW YORK

CONSTAB BALLADS
idually in 1912

titled THE DIALECT
POETRY OF CLAUDE McKAY published 1972
by arrangement with Mrs. Hope
McKay Virtue and Carl Cowl.

Preface to this edition copyright © 1972 by Wayne Cooper.

SONGS OF JAMAICA reprinted from a copy in
the Fisk University Library Negro Collection.

CONSTAB BALLADS reprinted from a copy in
the collections of The New York Public Library

INTERNATIONAL STANDARD BOOK NUMBER:
0-8369-8982-1

LIBRARY OF CONGRESS CATALOG CARD NUMBER:
73-38014

PRINTED IN THE UNITED STATES OF AMERICA

PREFACE TO THE 1972 EDITION

THIS excellent reprint of Claude McKay's early dialect poems is long overdue. Since independence, many Jamaicans have awakened to the importance of their native English dialect, both as language in its own right and as a vehicle most expressive of specifically Jamaican values.

Throughout long years of slavery and colonial dependency, the vigor of the dialect betrayed the common people's essential unity, desire for justice and unassuming humanity—impulses not transmuted to Jamaicans through the language and customs of their former masters, but ideals which blacks had possessed in Africa. These smoldering coals they jealously guarded and fanned back to life in the hills of Jamaica. Even as they forged a new culture in their island environment, they preserved through the dialect a durable link to their African origins. Into it they incorporated West African words, phrases, syntax and rhythm, as well as a treasury of African folk tales, the Annancy stories. Despite all efforts by British colonialists to obliterate memories of Africa from the black Jamaican consciousness, the dialect assured their survival. Jamaicans today are incomparably richer for it.

PREFACE TO THE 1972 EDITION

Claude McKay was among the first to embrace the dialect as a legitimate means of literary expression. He was born September 15, 1889, of black peasant origins in the hills of Clarendon Parish, Jamaica's south central "breadbasket". As a young man he met an unusual Englishman, Walter Jekyll, a dedicated student of Jamaica dialect, who had adopted Jamaica as his home. Jekyll had published in 1907 a collection of Annancy stories, digging sings, dancing tunes and ring tunes entitled JAMAICAN SONG AND STORY, now recognized as an early classic in the field.[1] Under Jekyll's patronage and guidance,[2] McKay produced in 1912 two volumes of his own dialect poetry, SONGS OF JAMAICA and CONSTAB BALLADS, which represented pioneering efforts by a modern, native born Jamaican to utilize the language of his people in portraying their life and thought. As such they claim today an important place in the development of Jamaican and West Indian literature.

Moreover, they are of great interest to students of black literature in the United States and elsewhere. The French critic, Jean Wagner, for example, noted the sharp contrast between McKay's use of the Jamaican dialect and P. L. Dunbar's use of the southern Negro dialect: "Here we are far from the dialect of the Dunbar school, inherited from the whites who had forged it to perpetuate the stereotype of Negro inferiority, and to fix them in their role of buffoons charged with amusing the white race . . . All things being equal, McKay's portrait of the Jamaican peasant is in substance that of the peasant the world over: profoundly attached to the earth, working the soil with a knowledge gained from age-long habit . . .

the Jamaican, like his counterpart the world over, is condemned to exploitation."[3]

These early works, furthermore, are related to McKay's later career in the United States and Europe. When they appeared he was only twenty-three—at the beginning of a long and turbulent literary life. That same year—1912 —McKay came to the United States to study agronomy, first at Tuskegee Institute, later at Kansas State College. He intended to return to Jamaica to serve his people, but, once in the United States, he was caught up in the larger struggle for social and racial justice. He never returned to his homeland.

McKay came to New York City in 1914 where he identified himself with the left-wing literati of Greenwich Village. In London in 1919, he published SPRING IN NEW HAMPSHIRE (1920), his first volume of verse in standard English. He returned to New York in 1921 to serve briefly as co-editor of THE LIBERATOR, then America's leading journal of avant-garde politics and art. The following year he published his fourth volume of poetry, HARLEM SHADOWS (1922) which heralded the Harlem Renaissance, a major literary awakening among black Americans in the 1920's. In his American verse, he leaned heavily upon the sonnet form and often echoed the Nineteenth Century English Romantics. Nevertheless, his forthright expression of the black man's anger, alienation, and rebellion against white racism introduced into modern American Negro poetry an articulate militancy of theme and tone which grew increasingly important with time.

PREFACE TO THE 1972 EDITION

Late in 1922, McKay travelled to Russia and thereafter lived for twelve years in Western Europe and North Africa. While abroad he published four volumes of fiction: HOME TO HARLEM (1928), BANJO (1929), GINGERTOWN (1932), and BANANA BOTTOM (1933). He was concerned, in all these works, with examining the place of the black man in the modern world. From 1934 to his death in 1948 he lived in the United States and published two more volumes, an autobiography entitled A LONG WAY FROM HOME (1937), and a study of HARLEM, NEGRO METROPOLIS (1940).

McKay drifted far from Jamaica and in fact became an American citizen in 1940. Nevertheless, the key to his literary and political development can be found in these dialect poems, where he first began to grapple with the twin problems of alienation and identity, constant themes of his later poetry and fiction. He had been educated to regard himself as a "black Briton" and he paid ample hommage in these poems to British imperialist values and attitudes. His evident deep immersion in English Romantic tradition, however, is tempered by a somewhat contradictory Victorian rationalism as expressed in the popular Social Darwinist doctrines of the period.

He tried to remain faithful to the black peasantry while simultaneously proclaiming his attachment to British traditions. Thus he betrayed not only a youthful naiveté but also a deep ambivalence toward Jamaican colonial society. His brief stint in the island constabulary only increased his emotional tensions, and brought him near to rebellion. Under the influence of Walter Jekyll he

PREFACE TO THE 1972 EDITION

sought escape in such Romantic pessimists as Leopardi and Schopenhauer and gloomily proclaimed the inevitability of life's injustices. Social-Darwinist thinking only deepened the pessimism of these poems. The black man's lowly status appeared predetermined by nature's inexorable laws. His natural urge to rebellion was here deflected but not subdued.

Once in the United States, however, he encountered a racial caste system that dispensed entirely with the social niceties that mask British racial prejudices. He could no longer echo clichés of Romantic disillusionment. Instead he began to harken back to older Romantic traditions, of rebellion and revolution. By World War I he was free to concentrate on the actual struggles and hopes of the black man in the midst of Western society.

SONGS OF JAMAICA and CONSTAB BALLADS are important today not merely as literary and linguistic creations, but as social documents. They are here combined in one volume and reprinted in their entirety for the first time in fifty years. It is our good fortune that once again they are accessible to the general public.

WAYNE COOPER

[1]See Jekyll, Walter, editor, JAMAICAN SONG AND STORY: *Annancy Stories, Digging Sings, Dancing Tunes, and Ring Tunes* (New York: Dover Publications, Inc., 1966). A new edition with introductory material by Philip Sherlock, Louise Bennett and Rex Nettleford.
[2]For sketches of Jekyll and an indication of his influence

on McKay, see his obituary in THE HANDBOOK OF JAMAICA (Kingston: 1930) 556-7; and McKay, Claude, MY GREEN HILLS OF JAMAICA (unpublished manuscript in the Schomberg Collection, New York City). Squire Gensir in BANANA BOTTOM is a fictionalized portrait of Jekyll.

[3]Wagner, Jean, LES POÈTES NÈGRES DES ÉTATS-UNIS (Paris: Librairie Istra, 1963) 220.

SONGS OF JAMAICA

BY

CLAUDE McKAY

WITH AN INTRODUCTION BY WALTER JEKYLL

Volume I

PREFACE

WHAT Italian is to Latin, that in regard to English is the negro variant thereof. It shortens, softens, rejects the harder sounds alike of consonants and vowels ; I might almost say, refines. In its soft tones we have an expression of the languorous sweetness of the South : it is a feminine version of masculine English ; pre-eminently a language of love, as all will feel who, setting prejudice aside, will allow the charmingly naïve love-songs of this volume to make their due impression upon them. But this can only happen when the verses are read aloud, and those unacquainted with the Jamaican tongue may therefore welcome a few hints as to pronunciation.

As a broad general direction, let it be observed that the vowels have rather the continental than the English sounds, while in the matter of the consonants the variation from English is of the nature of a pretty lisp.

The exact values of the vowels cannot, of course, be described, but they approximate on the whole more to those of Italy and France than to those

5

of England. One sound, that of *aw*, is entirely rejected, and *ah* is substituted for it. Thus *bawl*, *law*, *call*, *daughter*, etc., become *bahl*, *lah*, *cahl*, *dahter*, etc.

In the word *whe'*, which sometimes means *where* and sometimes *which*, the *e* has the same sound as in the word *met*. *Deh* is similarly pronounced, and the *e* is quite a short one, the *h* being added merely to distinguish *deh* from *de* (the). This short *e* often takes the place of the close English *a*, as in *tek* (take), *mek* (make).

My is almost invariably pronounced with a short *y*, and, to remind the reader of this, it is constantly spelt *me*. *Fe*—generally meaning *to*, but sometimes *for*—matches this short *my* exactly. In *caan'* (can't) the *a* is doubled in order to ensure the pronunciation *cahn*.

It is difficult to convey the exact value of *do'n* (down), *groun'* (ground). There is a faint trace of *ng* at the end of these words, and they rhyme to *tongue* pronounced very shortly and with a dumber vowel sound.

Vowels are sometimes changed out of mere caprice, as it seems. Thus we have *ef* for *if*, *trimble* for *tremble*, *anedder* for *anudder* (another), *stimulent* for *stimulant*, *a*—pronounced short—for *I*, *sperit* for *spirit*.

In *ya*, originally meaning *d'you hear*—but now thrown in just to fill up, like the *don't you know* of certain talkers—the *a* is a short *ah*.

We come now to the consonants. Bearing in

mind what was said above of the pretty lisp, let the *d* so often—generally, we may say—substituted for *th*, be of the very softest, as it were a *th* turning towards *d*, or to put it in another way, a lazily pronounced *th*. The negro has no difficulty whatever in pronouncing it clearly: it is merely that he does not, as a rule, take the trouble to do so. In these poems *the*, *they*, *there*, *with*, etc., are not always written *de*, *dey*, *dere*, *wid*, etc. ; and the reader is at liberty to turn any soft *th* into *d*, and any *d* into soft *th*. And here let me remark, in passing, that in one breath the black man will pronounce a word in his own way, and in the next will articulate it as purely as the most refined Englishman. Where the substitution of *d* makes the word unrecognisable, as in *moder* (mother), *oders* (others), the spelling *mudder*, *udders* is resorted to ; and for fear of confusion with well-known words, *though*, *those* are always written thus, although generally pronounced, *dough*, *dose*.

As *d* supplants the soft *th*, so does a simple *t* supplant the hard one ; as in *t'ing*, *not'ing* (or *nuttin'*,—for the *g* in words of two or more syllables is very commonly left out), *t'ink*, *t'ick*, *t'rough*, *met'od*, *wutless* (worthless).

V tends to pass into *b*, as in *lub* (love), *hab*, *lib*, *ebery*, *neber*, *cultibation*. *Vex*, though so written for the most part, is pronounced either with a decided *b* or with some compromise between that and *v*.

Of elisions, the commonest is that of the initial *s* when followed by another consonant. Thus *start*, *spread, stop, scrape, spoil, sting, skin*, etc., become *'tart, 'pread, 'top, 'crape, 'poil, 'ting, 'kin*, etc.

Final *d's* are often dropped, as in *lan', t'ousan', please'* (pleased) and other past participles, *min', chil'*—in these let care be taken to keep the long sound of the *i—wul'* (world), *wud* (word), *en'*.

Final *t's* also; as in *breas', cas', 'gains'* (against), *i'* (it), *las', wha', wus'* (worst), *tas'e* (taste).

Present participles, *passin', brukin'* (breaking), *outpourin'*, etc., lose their *g's*; and final *k's* sometimes disappear, as in *tas'*. *R's*, too, as in *you'* for *your, mo'* for *more, befo'* or simply *'fo'* for *before:* and they are even thrown out from the middle of words, as in *wuk* (work), *tu'n* (turn), *wud* (word). *Will* occasionally loses its *l's* and becomes *wi'*.

Initial vowels have also a habit of vanishing: as in *'bout* (about), *'long* (along), *'way* (away), *nuff* (enough), *'pon* (upon); but the elision of these and of longer first syllables is sometimes made up by tacking something to the end, and for *about, without, because* we get *'bouten, 'douten, 'causen.*

On the construction of the language it is unnecessary to dwell, for it is fully explained in the notes, and the reader will soon master the mysteries of *be'n* with its various significations, *is, was, were, have been, had been, did* (as sign of the past tense); of *deh*, which may be either an adverb (there) or an auxiliary verb as in *me deh beg* (I am begging); of *dem* tacked close to its noun, to show it is plural; of tenses apparently past which are present, and apparently present which are past: for the

unravelling of all which the needful help has, it
is hoped, been supplied by the notes aforesaid.

Readers of this volume will be interested to know
that they here have the thoughts and feelings of a
Jamaican peasant of pure black blood. The young
poet, aged twenty-two, spent his early years in the
depths of the country, and though he has now
moved to the more populous neighbourhood of
Kingston, his heart remains in his Clarendon hills.
He began life as a wheelwright, but the trade was
not to his mind, and he left it and enlisted in
the Constabulary.

WALTER JEKYLL.

CONTENTS

QUASHIE TO BUCCRA[1]

You tas'e[2] petater[3] an' you say it sweet,
But you no[4] know how hard we wuk[5] fe it;
You want a basketful fe quattiewut,[6]
'Cause you no know how 'tiff de bush fe cut.

De cowitch[8] under which we hab fe 'toop,
De shamar[9] lyin' t'ick like pumpkin soup,
Is killin' somet'ing[10] for a naygur man;
Much less[11] de cutlass workin' in we han'.

De sun hot like when fire ketch a[12] town;
Shade-tree look temptin', yet we caan' lie down,
Aldough we wouldn' eben ef we could,
Causen we job must finish soon an' good.[13]

---

[1] The buccra (white man), looking over the hedge at the black man's field, is addressed by the latter as follows.
[2] Taste.   [3] Sweet potato (*Ipomæa Batatas*).   [4] Don't.
[5] Work.   [6] Quattieworth: quattie, a quarter of sixpence.
[7] Because you don't know how stiff the bush is to cut, *i.e.*, what hard work it is to fell the trees and clear the land.
[8] *Mucuna pruriens.*
[9] Shamebush, the prickly sensitive plant (*Mimosa Pudica*).
[10] Terrible stuff.   [11] More.
[12] In.   [13] Because our job must be quickly and thoroughly done.

13

De bush cut done, de bank dem we deh dig,[1]
But dem caan' 'tan' sake o' we naybor pig;
For so we moul' it up he root it do'n,[2]
An' we caan' 'peak sake o' we naybor tongue.[3]

Aldough de vine is little, it can bear;
It wantin' not'in' but a little care:
You see petater tear up groun', you run,[4]
You laughin', sir, you must be t'ink a fun.[5]

De fiel' pretty?   It couldn't less 'an dat,[6]
We wuk de bes',[7] an' den de lan' is fat;
We dig de row dem eben in a line,
An' keep it clean—den so it *mus'* look fine.

You tas'e petater an' you say it sweet,
But you no know how hard we wuk fe it;
Yet still de hardship always melt away
Wheneber it come roun' to reapin' day.

---

[1] The clearing of the land done, we dig the banks—kind of terraces on the steep hill-side—but owing to our neighbour's pig they cannot stand.   "Bank dem"=banks.   This intrusive "dem" must be tacked closely to the preceding word.   It occurs again below—"row dem."

[2] For no sooner do we mould it up, than he (the pig) roots it (the bank) down.   "Down" is pronounced very short, and is a good rhyme to "tongue."

[3] And we cannot complain, for this would "bring confusion," *i.e.*, cause a row.

[4] A piece of humorous exaggeration: "When you see the potatoes tearing up the ground in their rapid growth you will run to save yourself from being caught and entangled in the vines."

[5] You are laughing, sir—perhaps you think I am exaggerating.

[6] Less than that=be otherwise.

[7] We work as well as we possibly can.

ME BANNABEES [1]

RUN ober mango trees,
  'Pread chock [2] to kitchen doo',
Watch de blue bannabees,
  Look how it ben' down low!

De blossom draw de bees
  Same how de soup draw man ; [3]
Some call it "broke-pot" peas,
  It caan' bruk we bu'n-pan. [4]

Wha' sweet so when it t'ick ? [5]
  Though some call it goat-tud, [6]
Me all me finger lick,
  An' yet no chew me cud. [7]

[1] A corruption of Bonavist, a climbing bean or pea.
[2] Right up.
[3] The blossom attracts bees, just as the soup made from the peas attracts man.
[4] It can't break our burn-pan—a tall saucepan.
[5] What is so good as this soup, when it is thick ?
[6] Goat-droppings—the name of a poisonous plant, somewhat resembling bannabees.
[7] Because I haven't yet got my belly full : see below.

15

A mumma plant[1] de root
  One day jes' out o' fun ;[2]
But now look 'pon de fruit,
  See wha' de "mek fun"[3] done.

I jam de 'tick dem 'traight
  Soon as it 'tart fe 'pread,[4]
An begin count de date
  Fe when de pod fe shed.[5]

Me watch de vine dem grow,
  S'er[6] t'row dung a de root :
Crop time look fe me slow,
  De bud tek long fe shoot.

But so de day did come,
  I 'crub de bu'n-pan bright,
An' tu'n down 'pon it[7] from
  De marnin' till de night.

An' Lard ! me belly swell,
  No 'cause de peas no good,
But me be'n tek[8] a 'pell
  Mo' dan a giant would.

Yet eben after dat
  Me nyam[9] it wid a will,
'Causen it mek me fat ;
  So I wi' lub it still.

---

[1] It was mamma who planted.
[2] With no serious purpose.
[3] To make fun = to trifle.
[4] As soon as it began to spread.
[5] When the pod will be formed.   [6] Sister.
[7] The soup.   [8] Did take.   [9] I ate.

Caan' talk [1] about gungu,[2]
 Fe me it is no peas ;
Cockstone [3] might do fe you,
 Me want me bannabees.

[1] It's not the least use your talking.
[3] Red peas—the beans of America.

[2] Congo peas.

LUB O' MINE

DARLIN', though you lub me still,
  I feel it so,
To t'ink dat we neber will
  Meet soon, you know ;

Eben when you tell me say [1]
  Dat your dear heart [2]
Did grow 'tronger ebery day
  An' hate fe part.

Feelin' all you' lub for me,
  I t'ink [3] you press
Your heart, as it use' to be, [4]
  Upon me breas'.

Lubin' you wid all me soul,
  De lub is such
Dat it beat out blood, [5]—de whole, [6]
  An' dat is much.

---

[1] Although you do tell me. The word 'say' is redundant.
[2] Love.   [3] Imagine.   [4] As formerly.
[5] Beats out relations—*i.e.*, makes relations nothing.
[6] Father and mother and all.

18

Lubin' you as you go 'long
 In a you walk ; [1]
Also when you chune [2] a song,
 An' as you talk.

An' a so I hate fe see [3]
 You go astray
In those t'ings dat you and me
 Can cast away. [4]

Lub, I dyin' [5] fe you' smile,
 An' some sweet news
Dat can cheer me heart awhile
 Fe wha' it lose.

Lub me, darlin'—lub, aldough
 You are now gone :
You can never leave me so—
 Friendless—alone.

---

[1] In your walk. [2] Tune = sing.
[3] And I so hate to sec. [4] Need not do. [5] I am dying.

TAKEN ABACK

LET me go, Joe, for I want go [1] home :
  Can't stan' wid you, [2]
  For pa might go [3] come ;
An' if him only hab him rum, [4]
I don't know whateber I'll do.

I must go now, for it's gettin' night
  I am afraid,
  An' 'tis not moonlight :
Give me de last hug, an' do it tight ;
Me pa gwin' go knock off me head. [5]

No, Joe, don't come !—you will keep me late,
  An' pa might be
  In him [6] sober state ;
Him might get vex' [7] an' lock up de gate,
Den what will becomin' of me ?

---

[1] To go.   [2] I can't stay with you.
[3] A redundant word, unaccented.
[4] If he chances to be in liquor.
[5] My papa is going to go (and) knock off my head. The
"going" is pronounced very short, making it sound like a *w*.
[6] His.   [7] Vexed.

Go wid *you*, Joe?—you don't lub me den !
  I shame'[1] o' you—
  Gals caan'[2] trust you men !
An' I b'en tekin' you fe me frien' ;[3]
Good-night, Joe, you've proven untrue.

[1] Am ashamed.   [2] Can't.
[3] And I've been taking you for my friend.

LITTLE JIM

Me Lard! me caan' bear it no mo'!
'Twill kill me dead, dis bad sore toe;
All day, all night, 'tis all de same,
Mek me a bawl out Massa name.[1]

O Lard o' me, a 'fraid[2] to tu'n,
De way de dreadful bluestone bu'n![3]
A[4] feel it movin' t'rough me j'ints,
Like million load o' needle-p'ints.

An' oh! me schoolmates dem[5] did laugh,
De day I nearly knock'[6] it off;
Me laugh meself fe sake o' shame,[7]
An' didn' know I'd go so lame.

I didna' then t'ink what I'd got[8]—
Good Lard, mumma, de bluestone hot![9]
I tell you, a wi' lose me head;[10]
You satisfy to kill me dead?[11]

---

[1] Making me bawl (pronounce *bahl*) out Massa's (God's) name.
[2] I am afraid.
[3] So dreadfully does the bluestone (sulphate of copper) burn.
[4] I.
[5] Redundant word   It is tacked closely to the preceding word.
[6] Knocked.   I laughed myself, out of bravado.
[7] I did not then picture to myself the extent of the injury.
[9] Is painful.   [10] I shall go out of my mind, I tell you.
[11] Can it be that you don't care whether you kill me or not?

An' oh! it is a double pain,
For I caan' go to school again,
To gellop ober fyahn [1] an' ditch,
An' 'crew de j'int o' teacher switch.[2]

No mo' roas' corn [3] fe little Jim,
Dem say dat it no good [4] fe him :
Me hide me face, for me caan' bear
To see dem passin' wid de pear.[5]

But me a don't a gwin' [6] to fret,
De half a toe wi' better get : [7]
I'll go to school once more, go bad ; [8]
Ay, it ease me a bit,[9] t'ank God !

---

[1] To gallop over fern.
[2] To screw the joint of teacher's switch, is to cut it so that it breaks when he uses it.
[3] Baked cob of green maize.   [4] They say it is not good.
[5] Alligator pear (*Persea gratissima*), not allowed to those suffering from wounds.   [6] But I am not going.
[7] The half toe will get well some day.
[8] Play the mischief; play tricks.   The *a* sounds as in French *la*.
[9] It is a bit easier.

JIM AT SIXTEEN

Corpy,[1] it pinch me so,
   De bloomin' ole handcuff;
A dunno warra mek [2]
   You put it on so rough.

Many a póliceman
   Hab come to dis before;
Dem slip same like a [3] me,
   An' pass t'rough lock-up door.[4]

Mumma, no bodder [5] cry,
   It should an [6] hotter be;
I wouldn' heed you when
   You use' [7] fe talk to me.

I run [8] away from you
   Same as I tu'n out school,[9]
'Caus'n a didn' want
   To stan' under no rule.[10]

---

[1] Corporal.   [2] I don't know what made.
[3] This intrusive "a" is common.   "Like" has the pronunciation of French *lac*.
[4] The door of the lock-up.
[5] Do not bother (trouble) to cry—*i.e.*, do not cry.
[6] Intrusive again.   [7] Used.   [8] Ran.
[9] As soon as I left school.   [10] To be under discipline.

An' though you send [1] fe me,
    A wouldn' face de home ;
Yet still dem [2] find you quick
    Same as de trouble come. [3]

Mumma, I know quite well
    You' lub fe me is 'trong ;
Yet still you don't a go
    Join wid me in a wrong. [4]

An' so I won't beg you
    To pay [5] fe me to-day ;
I'll bear me punishment, [6]
    'Twill teach me to obey.

*   *   *   *   *   *   *   *

Mumma, you' Jim get 'way
    An' come back home [7] to you,
An' ask [8] you to forgive
    Him all o' whe' him do. [9]

I want you to feget
    Dat I disgrace de name,
An' cause de ole fam'ly [10]
    To look 'pon me wid shame.

You come an' beg de judge
    Before dem call fe me, [11]
An' walk by de back gate,
    T'inkin' I wouldn' see.

---

[1] Sent.   [2] The police.   [3] When the trouble came.
[4] You are not going to back me up in wrongdoing.
[5] The fine.   [6] And go to prison.
[7] Has got off and comes home.   [8] Asks.
[9] All he has done. Whe' = what.   [10] Pronounce *fahmly*.
[11] You came and begged the magistrate before my case was brought
on.

But 'fore him let me go,
   Him lectur' me, mumma,
Tellin' me how I mus'
   Try no fe bruk de law.[1]

Mumma, I feel it, but
   No eye-water caan' drop :
Yet I wish dat it could,
   For me breat' partly 'top.[2]

So, mumma, I come back
   Again to be your boy,
An' ever as before
   To fill you' heart wid joy.

NOTE BY THE AUTHOR.—On Friday I went to Court on duty for the third time since my enlistment. I happened to escort a prisoner, a stalwart young fellow, and as I was putting on the handcuff, which was rather small, it pinched him badly, making a raw wound. And yet he was so patient, saying he knew that I could not help it. Although it was accidentally done, I felt so sad and ashamed. The above poem grew out of this incident.

[1] Telling me I must take care not to break the law. Pronounce *lah*.
[2] He means, that the lump in his throat is more painful than tears.

WHE' FE DO?[1]

LIFE will continue so for aye,
Some people sad, some people gay,
Some mockin'[2] life while udders pray ;
But we mus' fashion-out we way
An' sabe a mite fe rainy day—
      All we can do.

We needn' fold we han' an' cry,
Nor vex we heart wid groan and sigh ;
De best we can do is fe try
To fight de déspair drawin' nigh :
Den we might conquer by an' by—
      Dat we might do.

We hab to batter[3] in de sun,
An' dat isn't a little fun,
For Lard ! 'tis hellish how it bu'n :
Still dere's de big wul' to live do'n —
      So whe' fe do ?

---

[1] What to do? — equivalent to "What can't be cured, must be endured." The e of whe' is the French é.
[2] Making mock at.   [3] Labour and sweat ; swink.

We nigger hab a tas'¹ fe do,
To conquer prejudice dat ² due
To obeah,³ an' t'ings not a few
Dat keep we progress back fe true ⁴—
      But whe'' fe do?

We've got to wuk wid might an' main,
To use we han' an' use we brain,
To toil an' worry, 'cheme an' 'train ⁵
Fe t'ings that bring more loss dan gain ;
To stan' de sun an' bear de rain,
An' suck we bellyful o' pain
Widouten cry ⁶ nor yet complain—
      For dat caan'⁷ do.

And though de wul' is full o' wrong,
Dat caan' prevent we sing we song
All de day as we wuk along—
      Whe' else fe do?

We happy in de hospital ; ⁸
We happy when de rain deh fall ;
We happy though de baby bawl
Fe food dat we no hab at all ; ¹⁰
We happy when Deat' angel call ¹¹
Fe full ¹² we cup of joy wid gall :
Our fait' in this life is not small—
      De best to do.

¹ Task.   ² That's.   ³ Sorcery and magic.
⁴ Very much.   ⁵ Scheme and strain.   ⁶ Without crying.
⁷ Can't=won't.
⁸ All the lines of this stanza end with the sound *ahl.*
⁹ Is falling.   ¹⁰ Don't have at all=haven't got.
¹¹ Death's angel calls.   ¹² Fill.

An' da's [1] de way we ought to live,
For pain an' such [2] we shouldn' grieve,
But tek de best dat Nature give—
    Da's whe' fe do.

God mek de wul' fe black an' white ;
We'll wuk on in de glad sunlight,
Keep toilin' on wid all our might,
An' sleep in peace when it is night :
We must strive on to gain de height,
Aldough it may not be in sight ;
An' yet perhaps de blessed right
Will never conquer in de fight—
      Still, whe' fe do ?

We'll try an' live as any man, [3]
An' fight de wul' de best we can,
E'en though it hard fe understan'
    Whe' we mus' do.

For da's de way o' dis ya wul' ; [4]
It's snap an' bite, an' haul an' pull,
An' we all get we bellyful—
    But whe' fe do ?

---

[1] That's.   [2] The like.
[3] As others do, who make a good fight.   [4] Of this (here) world.

KING BANANA

GREEN mancha[1] mek[2] fe naygur man ;
   Wha' sweet so when it roas'?
Some boil it in a big black pan,
   It sweeter in a toas'.[3]

A buccra fancy[4] when it ripe,
   Dem use it ebery day ;
It scarcely give dem belly-gripe,
   Dem eat it diffran' way.[5]

Out yonder see somoke[6] a rise,
   An' see de fire wicket ;[7]
Deh go'p to heaben wid de nize[8]
   Of hundred t'ousan' cricket.

De black moul' lie do'n quite prepare'
   Fe feel de hoe an' rake ;
De fire bu'n, and it tek care
   Fe mek de wo'm[9] dem wake.

[1] Corruption of " Martinique," the best variety of banana in Jamaica.
[2] Is (or was) made.
[3] In a toast=toasted.   A toasted or roasted banana is a baked banana.
[4] It is buccra's fancy, *i.e.*, the white man likes it.
[5] In a different way : not so much at a time as we eat.
[6] This lengthening of a monosyllable into a dissyllable is common.
[7] Wicked.
[8] It goes up to heaven with the noise, etc. This is an excellent simile, as those acquainted with tropical crickets will know.
[9] Worms, *i.e.*, grubs.

30

Wha' lef' fe buccra teach again
  Dis time about plantation ?
Dere's not'in' dat can beat de plain
  Good ole-time cultibation.

Banana dem fat all de same [1]
  From bunches big an' 'trong ;
Pure nine-han' bunch a car' de fame,[2]—
  Ole met'od all along.

De cuttin' done same ole-time way,
  We wrap dem in a trash,[3]
An' pack dem neatly in a dray
  So tight dat dem can't mash.

We re'ch : [4] banana finish sell ; [5]
  Den we 'tart back fe home :
Some hab money in t'read-bag [6] well,
  Some spen' all in a rum.

Green mancha mek fe naygur man,
  It mek fe him all way ; [7]
Our islan' is banana lan',
  Banana car' de sway.[8]

[1] In spite of primitive methods of cultivation the bananas are just as plump.

[2] The nine-hand and only (pure) nine-hand bunches—none smaller, that is—grown by this old method have a fine reputation.

[3] In trash. Any refuse is called "trash." Here dried banana leaves are meant.

[4] Reach our journey's end.   [5] The selling of the bananas is over.

[6] Bag secured by a thread (string) round the mouth.

[7] In every way. He can eat it or sell it.

[8] Carries the sway, *i.e.*, is Jamaica's mainstay.

PLEADING

IF you lub me, Joanie, only tell me, dear,
    Do not be so cold
    When my lub is bold ;
Do not mek dis burnin' heart o' mine get drear,
    Tek it for your own,
    For 'tis yours alone.

I hab eber lub'd you from I saw[1] your face
    On dat Monday morn
    'Mongst de peas an' corn :
Lightly did you trip along wid yout'ful grace,
    Wid de kerchief red
    Wound about your head.

Durin' de revival[2] we b'en use' fe pray,
    Spirit we b'en hab,
    How we use' fe sob !
Yet how soon did all of it from we get 'way ![3]
    Lub kiver de whole,
    We feget we " soul."

---

[1] From the moment that I saw.
[2] At revival meetings those who " have the Spirit " give grunting sobs.
[3] Go away, pass away.

Though I could'n' see you when you younger b'en,
  It was better so,
  For we older grow,
An' I can protect you now from udder men,
  If you'll only be
  Fe me one,[1] Joanie.

How I saw you proudly draw up to your height—
  As we strolled along
  Gay in laugh an' song,
Passin' by de peenies [2] sheddin' greenish light—
  'Cos my lips did miss,[3]
  Stealin' one lee [4] kiss !

'Member you de days down by de river-side,
  I prevented you
  Your washin' to do,
Teasin' you at times till you got vex' an' cried,
  An' I try de while
  To coax you fe smile ?

Joanie, when you were me own a [5] true sweetheart,
  I lived in de air
  'Douten [6] t'ought of care,
Thinkin', O me Joan, dat' nuttin' could we [7] part,
  Naught to mek me fear
  Fe me own a dear.

When in church on Sunday days we use' fe sit,
  You dressed in light pink,
  How we used fe wink !
Wha' de parson say we cared for not a bit,
  Nuttin' could remove
  Our sweet t'oughts from love.

---

[1] Mine alone. [2] Fire-flies. [3] Make a mistake. [4] Little.
[5] There is a delicious caressing sound about this intrusive "a."
[6] Withouten, without. [7] Us.

I am thinkin', Joanie, when de nights were lone,
  An' you were afraid
  Of each darkened shade,
An' I use' fe guide you over river-stone,[1]
  How you trusted me
  Fe care[2] you, Joanie.

'Member you de time when many days passed by,
  An' I didn' come
  To your hill-side home,
How you wrote those sad, sad letters to know
   why,
  Till I comfort gave
  To my Joanie brave?

In those happy days, me Joan, you loved me
   then,
  An' I t'ought dat you
  Would be ever true ;
Never dreamed you would forsake me for strange
   men,
  Who caan' lub you so
  Much as thrown-up Joe.

Joanie, fickle Joanie, give up Squire's son ;
  You wi' soon hate him
  An' his silly whim,
An' your heart wi' yearn fe me when I am gone ;
  So, 'fo' 'tis too late,
  Come back to your mate.

[1] The stepping stones in the river. [2] Look after.

Joanie, when you're tired of dat worthless man,
 You can come back still
 Of your own free will :
Nummo[1] girl dis true, true heart will understan' ;
 I wi' live so-so,[2]
 Broken-hearted Joe.

An', Joan, in de days fe come I know you'll grieve
 For de foolishniss
 Dat you now call bliss :
Dere's no wrong you done me I would not forgive ;
 But you choice[3] your way,
 So, me Joan, good-day !

[1] No other girl can understand.   [2] Alone.
[3] Choose, have chosen.

THE BITER BIT

["Ole woman a swea' fe eat calalu :[1] calalu a swea' fe wuk
him[2] gut."—JAMAICA PROVERB.]

CORN an' peas growin' t'ick an' fas'
Wid nice blade peepin' t'rough de grass ;
An' ratta[3] from dem hole a peep,
T'ink all de corn *dem* gwin' go reap.

Ole woman sit by kitchen doo'
Is watchin' calalu a grow,
An' all de time a t'inking dat
She gwin' go nyam dem when dem fat.[4]

But calalu, grow'n' by de hut,
Is swearin' too fe wuk him gut ;
While she, like some, t'ink[5] all is right
When dey are in some corner tight.

Peas time come roun'[6]—de corn is lef' ;
An' ratta now deh train himse'f
Upon de cornstalk dem a' night
Fe when it fit to get him bite.[7]

[1] Spinach.　　　[2] His=her.　　　[3] The rats.　　　[4] Juicy.
[5] Thinks ; but it also means "think," and so equally applies to the
plural subject.　　　[6] The time for harvesting the peas arrives.
[7] And (every) rat now practises climbing the cornstalks at night, so
that he may get his bite when the corn is ripe.

De corn-piece lie do'n all in blue,[1]
An' all de beard dem floatin' too
Amongst de yellow grain so gay,[2]
Dat you would watch dem a whole day.

An' ratta look at ebery one,
Swea'in' dat dem not gwin' lef' none ;[3]
But Quaco know a t'ing or two,
An' swear say[4] dat dem won't go so.

So him go get a little meal
An' somet'ing good fe those dat steal,
An' mix dem up an' 'pread dem out
For people possess fas' fas' mout'.[5]

Now ratta, comin' from dem nes',
See it an' say " Dis food is bes' ; "
Dem nyam an' stop, an' nyam again,
An' soon lie do'n, rollin' in pain.

[1] This refers to the bluish leaf of the maize.
[2] Supply "all this makes so pretty a picture."
[3] They are not going to leave any.
[4] " Say" is redundant : it is tacked closely to " swear."
[5] For those who are too quick with their mouths.

OUT OF DEBT

De Christmas is finish';
It was rather skinnish,[1]
Yet still we are happy, an' so needn' fret,
For dinner is cookin',
An' baby is lookin'
An' laughin'; she knows dat her pa owe no debt.

De pas' hab de debtor,[2]
An' we cannot get her[3]
To come back an' grin at us as in time gone:
Dere's no wine fe breakfas',[4]
An' no one fe mek fuss,
We all is contented fe suck one dry bone.

No two bit o' brater[5]
Wid shopkeeper Marter,
I feel me head light sittin' down by me wife;
No weight lef' behin' me
No gungu[6] a line fe
De man who was usual[7] to worry me life.

[1] The fare was rather meagre.
[2] We were in debt last Christmas, but now we are free.
[3] The past.   [4] The midday meal.
[5] Shopkeeper Marter and I are no longer two brothers: meaning, I am not always going into his shop, and so keeping in debt. Pronounce *brahter*.
[6] Friends plant their gungu (Congo peas) together, and, in picking the crop, are not particular about the line between their properties. When they cease to be friends, they have *no gungo a line*. The phrase is equivalent to " to have no truck with."
[7] Pronounce without sounding the second *u*. Was usual = used.

OUT OF DEBT

We're now out o' season,[1]
  But dat is no reason
Why we shan't be happy wid heart free and light:
  We feel we are better
  Dan many dat fetter
Wid burden dey shoulder to mek Christmas bright.

  Some 'crape out de cupboard,
  Not 'memberin' no wud[2]
Dat say about fégettin' when rainy day:
  It comes widout warning
  'Fo' daylight a[3] marnin',
An', wakin', de blue cloud ta'n black dat was gay.

  De days dat gwin' follow
  No more will be hollow,
Like some dat come after de Christmas before:
  We'll lay by some money
  An' lick at de honey,[4]
An' neber will need to lock up our front door.[5]

  Jes'[6] look at de brightness
  Of dat poor an' sightless
Old man on de barrel a playin' de flute:
  Wha' mek him so joyful?
  His lap is of toy full,
A pick'ninny play wid de patch on his suit.

[1] Past Christmas.
[2] Entirely oblivious of the proverb (word) which tells us not to forget to make provision for the rainy day.
[3] In the.   [4] Enjoy the pleasure it brings.
[5] Against the bailiff.   [6] Just.

Ours too de same blessin',
An' we've learn' a lesson
We should have been learnin' from years long ago
A Christmas 'dout pleasure [1]
Gave dat darlin' treasure, [2]
An' duty to Milly is all dat we owe.

[1] Without pleasure, *i.e.*, a sober and quiet Christmas.
[2] Our little pickny.

THE HERMIT

FAR in de country let me hide myself
From life's sad pleasures an' de greed of pelf,
Dwellin' wid Nature primitive an' rude,
Livin' a peaceful life of solitude.

Dere by de woodland let me build my home
Where tropic roses[1] ever are in bloom,
An' t'rough de wild cane[2] growin' thick and tall
Rushes in gleeful mood de waterfall.

Roof strong enough to keep out season rain,[3]
Ur.der whose eaves loved swallows will be fain
To build deir nests, an' deir young birdlings rear
Widouten have de least lee t'ought of fear.[4]

An' in my study I shall view de wul',
An' learn of all its doin's to de full ;
List to de woodland creatures' music sweet—
Sad, yet contented in my lone retreat.

[1] In Jamaica any showy or sweet flower is called a rose.
[2] *Arundo Donax.*
[3] The heavy rains of May and October are called "season rains."
[4] Without having the smallest (least little) thought of fear.

FETCHIN' WATER

Watch how dem touris' like fe look
  Out 'pon me little daughter,
Wheneber fe her tu'n [1] to cook
  Or fetch a pan of water :
      De sight look gay ;
      Dat is one way,
      But I can tell you say,[2]
'Nuff rock'tone in de sea, yet none
But those 'pon lan' know 'bouten sun.[3]

De pickny comin' up de hill,
  Fightin' wid heavy gou'd,[4]
Won't say it sweet [5] him, but he will
  Complain about de load :
      Him feel de weight,
      Dem [6] watch him gait ;
      It's so some of de great
High people fabour t'ink [7] it sweet
Fe batter [8] in de boilin' heat.

[1] It is her turn.   [2] The "say" is redundant.
[3] In allusion to the Jamaica proverb, "Rock'tone (stone) a river bottom no feel sun hot."
[4] Struggling under his head-load—a gourd (calabash) filled with water.
[5] Is agreeable to.   [6] The tourists watch his upright carriage.
[7] Favour think = seem to think.
[8] Labour and sweat ; toil and moil.

Dat boy wid de karásene[1] pan,
   Sulky down to him toe,
His back was rollin' in a san',[2]
    For him pa mek him crow :[3]
       Him feel it bad,
       Near mek him mad,
       But teach him[4] he's a lad ;
Go disobey him fader wud,[5]
When he knows dat his back would sud ![6]

But Sarah Jane she wus 'an all,
   For she t'row 'way[7] de pan,
An' jam her back agains' de wall
    Fe fight her mumma Fan :
       Feelin' de pinch,
       She mek a wrinch
       An' get 'way ; but de wench
Try fe put shame upon her ma,
Sày dat she cook de bittle raw.[8]

Dis water-fetchin' sweet dem though
   When day mek up dem min',
An' 'nuff o' dem 'tart out fe go,
    An' de weader is fine :
       De pan might leak,
       Dem don't a 'peak,
       Nor eben try fe seek
Some clay or so[9] to mek it soun' ;
Dem don't care ef dem wet all roun'.

The favourite receptacle for water is a four-gallon kerosene tin (pan).
[2] In the sand.   [3] Cry out.   [4] But it will teach him.
[5] What?—disobey his father's orders?   [6] Get a lathering.
[7] Threw down.
[8] Said that she cooked the victual raw, *i.e.*, only half cooked it.
[9] Or something.

Dén all 'bout de road dem 'catter
  Marchin' álong quite at ease ;
Dat time listen to deir chatter,
  Talkin' anyt'ing dem please :
      Dem don't a fear,
      Neider a care,
      For who can interfere ?
T'ree mile—five, six tu'n,[1]—an' neber [2]
W'ary, but could do it [3] for eber.

---

[1] Turns, *i.e.*, journeys to the spring and back.
[2] For rhythm, read thus : T'ree mile —five, six —tu'n, an'—neber.
[3] Pronounce *dweet*.

SCHOOL-TEACHER NELL'S
LUB-LETTER

IF you promise to lub me alway,
   I will foreber be true,
An' you don't mek me sorry [1] de day
   Dat I give myself to you.

How I 'member de night when we meet,[2]
   An' chat fe de first time of lub !
I go home, an' den neber could eat
   None o' de plateful o' grub.

An' de day it was empty to me,
   Wakin', but dreamin' of you,
While de school it was dull as could be,
   An' me hate me wuk fe do.[3]

Oh, I knew of your lub long before
   My school friends tell [4] me of it,
And I watch at you from de school door,
   When you pass to de cockpit.[5]

[1] Make me regret.   [2] How well I remember the night we met.
[3] I hated the doing of my work.   [4] Told.
[5] A natural depression in the ground, in the vicinity of the author's
home, bears this name.

Den I hear too dat you use' fe talk,
 Say,[1] if you caan' ketch me dark night,
You would sure ketch me as me deh walk [2]
 In a de [3] open moonlight.

An' you' wud come to pass [4] very soon,
 For scarcely a mont' did gone
When de light of de star an' de moon
 Shine [5] bright as we kiss all alone.

I can neber remember de times
 Ma scolded her little Nell ; [6]
All day her tongue wuks like de chimes
 Dat come from de old school-bell.

I have given up school-life fe you :
 Sweetheart, my all [7] is your own ;
Den say you will ever be true,
 An' live fe you' Nellie alone.

[1] Used to (talk and) say.
[2] You would be sure to catch me as I walked.   [3] In the.
[4] And your word came to pass.   [5] Shone.
[6] I cannot count the number of scoldings I have had from mamma.
[7] Whole self.

NELLIE WHITE

(AN ANSWER TO THE FOREGOING)

SWEETHEART, I have loved you well,
More than dis lee tongue can tell,
An' you need not hab no fear,
For I'll marry you, my dear.

What are you talkin' about?
Don't say that I'll play you out;[1]
Swif' ole Time, me Nell, will prove
Dat 'tis you alone I love.

Cry not, except 'tis for joy ;
Can't you trus' dis big-heart boy?
Nell, I hate fe see you weep ;
Tek my heart, an' go to sleep.

How could I deceive you, Nell?
Don't I love you much too well?
Could I fool dat plump black cheek?
Don't cry, darlin'—look up—speak !

[1] False.

47

Nellie of the pretty feet
An' the palm-like shape so neat,
I have eyes to see but you ;
Darling, trust me to be true !

Nell, me dear, you need not fret,
For you are my food, my breat' ;
Trust me, trust me, Nellie White,
Kiss me, lee sweetheart—good-night !

RETRIBUTION

DE mule dem in de pasture an' de donkey 'pon red
    groun',[1]
An' we boys mus' ketch dem all befo' de evenin'
    sun go do'n ;
De tas'[2] it isn't easy for de whole o' dem can run,
          An' grass-lice[3] lie do'n set.[4]

Grass-lice dat mek you trimble long time[5] more
    dan when you meet
A. man dat mean to fight you who you know you
    cannot beat ;
Dem mek you feel you' blood crawl from you' head
    do'n to you' feet,
          An' wish dat you b'en[6] wet.

An', like a 'pite,[7] see all de mule a 'ketter t'rough de
    grass,
So chupidly a-followin' de foolish ole jackass ;
But when you hea' we ketch dem, we wi' serve dem
    such a sauce
          By ridin' dem to deat' !

---

[1] Poor patchy land with open spaces of red earth.   [2] Task.
[3] Small ticks.   [4] Waiting for us.   [5] Long time=much.
[6] Had been, were.   [7] As though to spite us.

We breat' is partly givin' out [1] as up de hill we go
    up ;
De beast dem seem to understan' say " Day longer
    'an rope," [2]
An' dat de night wi' come befo' we ketch dem is
    deir hope ;
               But we shall conquer yet.

For though dem t'ink dem hab some sense, dem
    all run right between
De rocky road above de swamp, where it hab ebe'r
    been
Our luck to nab dem in de trap dat neber can be
    seen
             By dem—Dey're in de net !

We hab dem pullin' on de bit as we race mile 'pon
    mile,
An' grass-lice in we back a crawl an' 'ting us all de
    while ;
But blood is drippin' from dem mout', 'twill teach
    dem not fe [3] vile,
          We'll race dem out o' breat'

---

[1] Three parts gone.
[2] Ro-op, in two syllables. The proverb means, " I'll be even with
you."   [3] To be.

TO E. M. E.

You see[1] me smile: but what is it?
A sweetened pain—a laughin' fit—
    A little honeyed dart,
    That, passing, stabs my heart,
Yet mek me glad a bit.

You see me dance: 'twas but my feet,
You should have heard my heart a beat!
    For none o' it was real:
    It be'n a priceless[2] sale
Of bitter for a sweet.

Dis laughin' face!—'tis full o' joy
Because it is a baby's toy;[3]
    But when de child is gone
    An' the darkness comes on,
'Twill be anudder boy.[4]

You hear me sing: what is de tune?
De song of one that's dyin' soon,
    A whirlin', tossin' life
    Flung on de wul' of strife;
I call it "debil's boon."

---

[1] Saw.   [2] Profitless.   [3] The speaker has a baby on his knee.
[4] I shall look very different.

51

De many pleasures? Wha's de gain?
I'll tell you of a grindin' pain
  Dat companies de birt',
  An' runs[1] wid vengeance[2] mirt'
De life, till it is slain.

Why do I sleep? My eyes know why,
Same how a life knows why it die : [3]
  Dey sleep on in distress,
  Knowin' not why dey res',
But feelin' why dey cry.

I'm hungry now, so eat once mo',
E'en though I'll soon be like befo' ;
  For, as in udder t'ings,
  De seemin' pleasure clings,
De cravin' has no cure.

It always seem so strange to me,
Dat *you* can satisfy[4] to be
  A life whose daily food
  Is pain : de only good,
Deat' dat will set it free.

---

[1] Chases, hunts.   [2] Vengeful.
[3] My eyes no more know why, than a life knows why it dies.
[4] Be content.

HARD TIMES

DE mo' me wuk, de mo' time hard,
    I don't know what fe do;
I ben' me knee an' pray to Gahd,
    Yet t'ings same as befo'.

De taxes knockin' at me door,
    I hear de bailiff's v'ice;
Me wife is sick, can't get no cure,
    But gnawin' me like mice.[1]

De picknies hab to go to school
    Widout a bite fe taste;
And I am working like a mule,
While buccra, sittin' in de cool,
    Hab 'nuff nenyam fe waste.[2]

De clodes is tearin' off dem back
    When money seems noa mek;
A man can't eben ketch a mac,[3]
    Care how him 'train him neck.[4]

---

[1] Trying to get money from me.   [2] Food and to spare.
[3] Shilling: short for macaroni.
[4] However hard he may strain his neck. "Care how "—I don't care
how,—no matter how.

De peas won't pop,[1] de corn can't grow,
  Poor people face[2] look sad ;
Dat Gahd would cuss de lan' I'd know,
  For black naygur too bad.

I won't gib up, I won't say die,
  For all[3] de time is hard ;
Aldough de wul' soon en', I'll try
My wutless[4] best as time goes by,
  An' trust on in me Gahd.

[1] Spring.   [2] People's faces.   [3] Although.
[4] Worthless: meaning, " I'll try my very best, poor as that may be."

CUDJOE FRESH FROM DE LECTURE

'Top *one* minute, Cous' Jarge, an' sit do'n 'pon de
    grass,
An' mek a [1] tell you 'bout de news I hear at las',
How de buccra te-day tek time an' bégin teach
All of us dat was deh [2] in a clear open speech.

You miss somet'ing fe true, but a wi' mek you
    know,
As much as how a can, how de business a go :
Him tell us 'bout we self, an' mek we fresh [3] again,
An' talk about de wul' from commencement to en'.

Me look 'pon me black 'kin, an' so me head grow
    big,
Aldough me heaby han' dem hab fe plug [4] an' dig ;
For ebery single man, no car' [5] about dem rank,
Him bring us ebery one an' put 'pon de same plank.

---

[1] Make I = let me.   [2] There.
[3] Over : meaning, "He gave us a new view of our origin, and
explained that we did not come from Adam and Eve, but by evolution."
[4] Plough, *i.e.*, pick up the ground with a pickaxe.
[5] Care : no matter what their rank.

Say, parson do de same?[1]   Yes, in a dift'ren' way,
For parson tell us how de whole o' we are clay ;
An' lookin' close at t'ings, we hab to pray quite
    hard
Fe swaller wha' him say an' don't t'ink bad o'
    Gahd.

But dis man tell us 'traight 'bout how de whole
    t'ing came,
An' show us widout doubt how Gahd was not fe
    blame ;
How change cause eberyt'ing fe mix up 'pon de eart',
An' dat most hardship come t'rough accident o'
    birt'.

Him show us all a sort[2] o' funny 'keleton,
Wid names I won't remember under dis ya sun ;
Animals queer to deat',[3] dem bone, teet', an' head-
    skull,
All dem so dat did live in a de ole-time wul'.

No 'cos say we get cuss mek fe we 'kin come so,
But fe all t'ings come 'quare, same so it was to go :[4]
Seems our lan'[5] must ha' been a bery low-do'n
    place,
Mek it tek such long time in tu'ning out a race.

---

[1] Do you say that parson does the same?
[2] All sorts.   [3] The queerest animals.
[4] It is not because we were cursed (Gen. ix. 25) that our skin is
dark ; but so that things might come square, there had to be black and
white.   [5] Africa.

Yes, from monkey we spring: I believe ebery
    wud;
It long time better dan f'go say we come from
    mud:
No need me keep back part, me hab not'in' fe
    gain;
It's ebery man dat born — de buccra mek it
    plain.

It really strange how some o' de lan' dem advance;
Man power in some ways is nummo soso chance;[1]
But suppose eberyt'ing could tu'n right upside
    down,
Den p'raps we'd be on top an' givin' some one
    houn'.[2]

Yes, Cous' Jarge, slabery hot fe dem dat gone
    befo':
We gettin' better times, for those days we no
    know;[3]
But I t'ink it do good, tek we from Africa
An' lan' us in a blessed place as dis a ya.[4]

Talk 'bouten Africa, we would be deh till now,
Maybe same half-naked—all day dribe buccra cow,
An' tearin' t'rough de bush wid all de monkey dem,
Wile an' uncibilise',[5] an' neber comin' tame.

[1] No more than pure chance.
[2] Hound: equivalent to the English slang phrase "giving some one beans."
[3] Do not know: have no experience of.   [4] This here.
[5] Wild and uncivilised.

I lef' quite 'way from wha' we be'n deh talk about,[1]
Yet still a couldn' help—de wuds come to me
    mout';
Just like how yeas' get strong an' sometimes fly de
    cark,[2]
Same way me feelings grow, so I was boun' fe talk.

Yet both horse partly [3] runnin' in de selfsame
    gallop,
For it is nearly so de way de buccra pull up:
Him say, how de wul' stan', dat right will neber be,
But wrong will eber gwon [4] till dis wul' en' fe we.

  [1] I have run right away from what we were talking about.
  [2] Makes the cork fly.   [3] Almost.   [4] Go on.

DE DAYS DAT ARE GONE

I T'INK of childhood days again,
  An' wish dat I was free
To res' me baby head once more
  Upon me mudder's knee :
If we had power to change dis life
  An' live it back again,
We would be children all de time
  Nor fret at childhood's pain.

I look on my school life of old,
  Dem sweet days dat are pas',
An' wonder how I'd wish [1] to see
  Those dear times en' at las' :
It was because I was a boy,
  An' knew not what b'en good ;
All time I tas'e de supple-jack, [2]
  Bein' I was so rude.

An' o' de marnings when I woke,
  'Fo' you can see you' han',
I mek me way on to de spring
  Fe full [3] me bucket-pan :
I t'ought ofttimes dat it was hard
  For me to wake so soon ;
Dere was no star fe light de way,
  Much more [4] de white roun' moon.

[1] I could wish.   [2] A cane.   [3] Fill.   [4] Less.

Still, childhood pain could neber las',
  An' I remember yet
De many sorrows 'cross me pat'[1]
  Dat neber mek me fret:
But now me joys are only few,
  I live because I'm boun',
An' try fe mek my life of use
  Though pain lie all aroun'.

[1] Across my path.

REVEILLE SOUN'IN'

REVEILLE ! de reveille soun',
  Depôt p'liceman mus' wake up ;[1]
Some mus' dress fe go to town,
  Some to Parade fe shake-up.[2]

You lazy ones can lay down still,
  We have no time fe dat ;
De wake-up[3] comin' roun', an' you'll
  Jump as you feel de cat.

For soon de half pas' dress[4] will blow
  Fe we to go a-drillin' ;
De time is bery short, an' so
  We mus' be quick an' willin'.

A marnin' bade is sweet fe true,[5]
  But we mus' quick fe done ;
It col' dough,[6] so it's only few
  Can stan' it how it bu'n.[7]

[1] Read thus : De—pôt p'lice—man mus'—wake up.   [2] Drill.
[3] The sergeant with his cane.   [4] The 5.30 bugle.
[5] A morning bathe is very, very delicious.   [6] It's cold though.
[7] Can stand the burning, *i.e.*, the chill.

'Tis quarter warnin'[1] soun'in' now,
  Our arms mus' clean an' soun' ;
We will ketch 'port[2] ef we allow
  A speck fe lodge aroun'.

Tip[3] blow yet? good Lard ! hear "fall in,"
  Must double 'pon de grass ;
I didn' know de las' call be'n
  Deh blow on us so fas'.

---

[1] The 5.45 bugle.   [2] Get reported.
[3] A short sharp bugle-call, to summon the men before the " fall in."

OLD ENGLAND

I've a longin' in me dept's of heart dat I can
    conquer not,
'Tis a wish dat I've been havin' from since I could
    form a t'o't,[1]
'Tis to sail athwart the ocean an' to hear de billows
    roar,
When dem ride aroun' de steamer, when dem beat
    on England's shore.

Just to view de homeland England, in de streets
    of London walk,
An' to see de famous sights dem 'bouten which
    dere's so much talk,
An' to watch de fact'ry chimneys pourin' smoke up
    to de sky,
An' to see de matches-children, dat I hear 'bout,
    passin' by.

I would see Saint Paul's Cathedral, an' would hear
    some of de great
Learnin' comin' from de bishops, preachin' relics
    of old fait';

[1] Thought.

63

I would ope me mout' wid wonder at de massive
  organ soun',
An' would 'train me eyes to see de beauty lyin'
  all aroun'.

I'd go to de City Temple, where de old fait' is
  a wreck,
An' de parson is a-preachin' views dat most folks
  will not tek;
I'd go where de men of science meet togeder in
  deir hall,
To give light unto de real truths, to obey king
  Reason's call.

I would view Westminster Abbey, where de great
  of England sleep,
An' de solemn marble statues o'er deir ashes vigil
  keep;
I would see immortal Milton an' de wul'-famous
  Shakespeare,
Past'ral Wordswort', gentle Gray, an' all de great
  souls buried dere.

I would see de ancient chair where England's
  kings deir crowns put on,
Soon to lay dem by again when all de vanity is
  done;
An' I'd go to view de lone spot where in peaceful
  solitude
Rests de body of our Missis Queen,[1] Victoria de
  Good.

[1] Always so called in Jamaica.

An' dese places dat I sing of now shall afterwards
    impart
All deir solemn sacred beauty to a weary searchin'
    heart;
So I'll rest glad an' contented in me min'[1] for
    evermore,
When I sail across de ocean back to my own
    native shore.

[1] Mind.

E

DAT DIRTY RUM

IF you *must* drink it, do not come
  An' chat up in my face ;
I hate to see de dirty rum,
  Much more to know de tas'e.

What you find dere to care about [1]
  I never understan' ;
It only dutty up you mout',
  An' mek you less a man.

I see it throw you 'pon de grass
  An' mek you want no food,
While people scorn you as dey pass
  An' see you vomit blood.

De fust beginnin' of it all,
  You stood up calm an' cool,
An' put you' back agains' de wall
  An' cuss our teacher fool. [2]

---

[1] To like.
[2] Abused our schoolmaster and called him a fool.   To "cuss" is to
"abuse" : to "cuss bad word" is to "swear."

66

You cuss me too de se'fsame day
    Because a say you wrong,[1]
An' pawn you' books an' went away
    Widout anedder song.[2]

Your parents' hearts within dem sink,
    When to your yout'ful lip
Dey watch you raise de glass to drink,
    An' shameless tek each sip.

I see you in de dancing-booth,
    But all your joy is vain,
For on your fresh an' glowin' youth
    Is stamped dat ugly stain.

Dat ugly stain of drink, my frien',
    Has cost you your best girl,
An' mek you fool 'mongst better men
    When your brain's in a whirl.

You may smoke just a bit indeed,
    I like de " white seal "[3] well ;
Aldough I do not use de weed,
    I'm fond o' de nice smell.

But wait until you're growin' old
    An' gettin' weak an' bent,
An' feel your blood a-gettin' cold
    'Fo' you tek stimulent.

---

[1] Because I said you were wrong.   [2] Without another word.
[3] The name of a brand of cigarettes.

Then it may mek you stronger feel
   While on your livin' groun' ; [1]
But ole Time, creepin' on your heel,
   Soon, soon will pull you down :

Soon, soon will pull you down, my frien',
   De rum will help her [2] too ;
An' you'll give way to better men,
   De best dat you can do. [3]

[1] While in this life.   [2] Time.
[3] Which is the best thing you can do.

HEART-STIRRINGS

You axe me as de bell begin fe 'trike,
Me Mikey, ef de wuk a didn' like;
De queshton, like de bell, soun' in me heart
Same how de anvil usual mek me 'tart.[1]

You's a chil'[2] an' know naught 'bout de wul' yet,
But you'll grow an' larn t'ings you won't feget;
You lub you' life, an' t'ink dere's nuttin' better,
Yet all you' pickny dream dem soon will 'ketter.[3]

Tek me advice ya, chil', an' as you grow
Don't choose a wuk dat you no like : aldough
You might see money in o' it, at lengt'
You will get tired o' it an' repent.

A suffer, but I t'ink it mek me wise;
It wasn' fe de money 'trike me yeyes,[4]
But "water mo' 'an flour"[5] is true wud,
An' eye-water run too long tu'n to blood.[6]

---

[1] Just as the sound of an anvil—the speaker was a blacksmith—
makes me start and arouses disagreeable recollections, so does your
question.   [2] Child.   [3] Scatter.

[4] It wasn't the attraction of the high wages.

[5] "Beggars can't be choosers." The reference is to dumplings made
with too much water.

[6] This means that he (the speaker) was unhappy at home.

Hard life caan' kill me, but annoyance might,
Me lub me right, an' fe it me wi' fight :
Me wi' lef' beef fe nyam an' choose cow-lung,
Fe sabe meself from an annoying tongue.[1]

But sometime', chil', you jump from fryin'-pan
'Traight in a fire ; an', try as you can,
You caan' come out, but always wishin' den
Fe get back in de fryin'-pan again.

Ole Buccra Dabis, libing easy life,
One night get mad an' kill himself an' wife ;
Den we hear t'ings we neber be'n know yet,
De buccra man was ears an' han's in debt.

Miss Laura lean back in her rockin'-chair
So sweet dat we might jes' t'ink she no care
'Bout naught ; yet some say dat 'cos she caan' get
Mas' Charley fe him husban'[2] she deh fret.

Dat's how life 'tan',[3] me chil' ; dere is somet'ing
Deep down in we dat you can neber bring
People, howeber wise, fe understan' :
Caan' feel man heart same how you feel dem han'.

Fe lub, me chil', lub wha' you natur' hate![4]—
You'll live in misery, prayin' hard fe fait',
Which won't come eben ef you 'crub you' knees
In fifty quart o' corn an' lady-peas.[5]

---

[1] Prov. xv. 17 ; xvii. 1. [2] Master Charley for her husband.
[3] Stands=is.
[4] If you try to make yourself love what your nature hates. This line
is partly an exclamation, partly an interrogation.
[5] Black-eye peas.

Fe hate a t'ing you whole min' come in one :
You try fe keep it[1] back much as you can,
But "flesh caan' conquer 'perit" Bible say,
You hab fe give it up,[2] an' den 'top pray.

Me carry hell, me chil', in a me ches',
Me laugh, me cry, me couldn' get no res' ;
Eat all de same an' neber fatter less[3]
Dan now, aldough me min' was so distress'.

An' though a feel it hard, a wouldn' fret ;
Me min' don't mek so, but it eber set
Fe conquer, yet it couldn' wash away
De t'oughts dem dat come 'tronger ebery day.

You 'stan',[4] me chil'? I caan' explain it mo' :
Life funny bad, so is de ways also ;
For what we t'ink is right is often wrong,
We live in sorrow as we journey 'long.

[1] The hatred.   [2] Give up trying.
[3] Less fat.   [4] Do you understand?

DE DOG-ROSE

Growin' by de corner-stone,[1]
  See de pretty flow'r-tree blows,
Sendin' from de prickly branch
  A lubly bunch o' red dog-rose.[2]

An' de bunch o' crimson red,
  Boastin' on de dark blue tree,
Meks it pretty, prettier yet
  Jes' as dat dog-rose can be.[3]

Young Miss Sal jes'[4] come from school:
  Freddy, fresh from groun' an' grub,
Pick de dog-rose off de tree,
  Gib Miss Sal to prove his lub.

Then I watch on as dem kiss
  Right aroun' de corner-stone,
An' my heart grow vex' fe see
  How dem foolish when alone.

An' I listen to deir talk,
  As dey say dey will be true ;
" Eber true " I hear dem pledge,
  An' dat naught can part dem two.

[1] Angle of the house.   [2] A dark red sweet-rose.
[3] Makes it pretty—as pretty as it is possible for a dog-rose to be.
[4] Just.

De petchary [1] laugh an' jig,
   Sittin' on a bamboo low ;
Seems him guess, jes' like mese'f
   How de whole t'ing gwin' fe go.

Time gwon,[2] an' de rose is not :
   I see Fred, wi' eyes all dim,
Huggin' up de corner-stone,
   For his love has jilted him ;

Left him for anedder man
   Wid a pile o' money,
Dat he carried from his land
   O' de Injin coney. [3]

Wonder whe' de petchary ?
   De rose-tree is dead an' gone ;
Sal sit in de big great-house,[4]
   Cooin' to her baby son.

[1] Grey king-bird.   [2] Goes on ; passes away.
[3] England or Scotland, the home of the Indian coney (common rabbit)—pronounced *cunny*.
[4] The principal house on a property is so called.

A MIDNIGHT WOMAN TO THE BOBBY

No palm me up,[1] you dutty brute,
You' jam mout' mash[2] like ripe bread-fruit;
You fas'n now, but wait lee ya,[3]
I'll see you grunt under de law.

You t'ink you wise,[4] but we wi' see;
You not de fus' one fas' wid me;
I'll lib fe see dem tu'n you out,
As sure as you got dat mash' mout'.

I born right do'n beneat' de clack[5]
(You ugly brute, you tu'n you' back?)
Don' t'ink dat I'm a come-aroun',[6]
I born right 'way in 'panish Town.

[1] Don't put your hands on me.   [2] Your d—d mouth is all awry.
[3] You are fast (meddling, officious) now, but wait a little, d'you hear?
[4] You think you're wise.
[5] The clock on the public buildings at Spanish Town.
[6] Day-labourers, men and women, in Kingston streets and wharves, famous for the heavy weights they carry, are called come-arounds.

Care how you try, you caan' do mo'
Dan many dat was hyah befo' ; [1]
Yet whe' dey all o' dem te-day ? [2]
De buccra dem no kick dem 'way ? [3]

Ko [4] 'pon you' jam samplatta [5] nose :
'Cos you wear Mis'r Koshaw clo'es [6]
You t'ink say you's de only man, [7]
Yet fus' time [8] ko how you be'n 'tan'. [9]

You big an' ugly ole tu'n-foot [10]
Be'n neber know fe wear a boot ;
An' chigger nyam you' tumpa toe, [11]
Till nit full i' like herrin' roe.

You come from mountain naked-'kin, [12]
An' Lard a mussy ! you be'n thin,
For all de bread-fruit dem be'n done,
Bein' 'poil' up by de tearin' sun : [13]

---

[1] No matter how you try, you can't do more than your predecessors (all that were here before).

[2] Yet where are they all to-day?

[3] Did not the buccra (white man) kick them away (dismiss them)?

[4] Look.

[5] A piece of leather cut somewhat larger than the size of the foot, and tied sandal-wise to it : said of anything that is flat and broad.

[6] Mr Kershaw's clothes, *i.e.*, police uniform. Col. Kershaw, Inspector-General of Police in 1911 (when this poem was written) and for many years before.

[7] A mighty fine fellow.   [8] When I knew you first.

[9] Look what sort of figure you cut.   [10] Turned-in foot.

[11] And chigoes (burrowing fleas) had eaten into your maimed toe, and nits (young chigoes) had filled it.

[12] Naked skin, *i.e.*, with your shirt and trousers full of holes.

[13] Having been spoilt by the hot sun. Pronounce "bein'" as a monosyllable.

De coco [1] couldn' bear at all,
For, Lard ! de groun' was pure white-marl ;
An' t'rough de rain part [2] o' de year
De mango tree dem couldn' bear.

An' when de pinch o' time you feel
A 'pur you a you' chigger heel,[3]
You lef' you' district, big an' coarse,
An' come join [4] buccra Police Force.

An' now you don't wait fe you' glass,[5]
But trouble me wid you' jam fas' ; [6]
But wait, me frien', you' day wi' come,
I'll see you go same lak a some.[7]

Say wha' ?—'res' me ? [8]—you go to hell !
You t'ink Judge don't know unno well ? [9]
You t'ink him gwin' go sentance [10] me
Widout a soul fe witness i' ?

[1] An edible root (*Colocasia antiquorum*).
[2] During some months.
[3] And when you felt hard times spurring you in your chigger-eaten heel.
[4] Came and joined.
[5] You don't wait for the right and proper moment.
[6] With all your infernal forwardness and officiousness.
[7] Same like some = just as others before you did.
[8] What's that ?—arrest me ?
[9] D'you think the magistrate doesn't know your tricks ? Unno or Onnoo is an African word, meaning " you " collectively.
[10] Pronounce the *a* ' ah,' but without accent.

MOTHER DEAR

"Husban', I am goin'—
Though de brooklet is a-flowin',
An' de coolin' breeze is blowin'
    Softly by ;
Hark, how strange de cow is mooin',
An' our Jennie's pigeons cooin',
While I feel de water [1] growin',
    Climbing high.

"Akee [2] trees are laden,
But de yellow leaves are fadin'
Like a young an' bloomin' maiden
    Fallen low ;
In de pond de ducks are wadin'
While my body longs for Eden, [3]
An' my weary breat' is gledin'
    'Way from you.

"See dem John-crows [4] flyin' !
'Tis a sign dat I am dyin' ;
Oh, I'm wishful to be lyin'
    All alone :

[1] The water of dropsy rising from the legs towards the heart.
[2] *Cupania sapida*, bearing beautiful red fruits.
[3] To English readers this and the next (gledin'=gliding) would hardly seem to be rhymes.   Nevertheless they are so.
[4] Turkey-buzzards.

77

Fait'ful husban', don't go cryin',
Life is one long self-denyin'
All-surrenderin' an' sighin'
            Livin' moan."

" Wife, de parson's prayin',
Won't you listen what he's sayin',
Spend de endin' of your day in
            Christ our Lord?"
But de sound of horses neighin',
Baain' goats an' donkeys brayin',
Twitt'rin' birds an' children playin'
            Was all she heard.

Things she had been rearin',
Only those could claim her hearin',
When de end we had been fearin'
            Now had come :
Now her last pain she is bearin',
Now de final scene is nearin',
An' her vacant eyes are starin'
            On her home.[1]

Oh ! it was heart-rendin'
As we watched de loved life endin',
Dat sweet sainted spirit bendin'
            To de death:
Gone all further hope of mendin',
With de angel Death attendin',
An' his slayin' spirit blendin'
            With her breath.

---

[1] The spot in the garden she had chosen for her burial-place.

KITE-FLYING

HIGHER fly, my pretty kite,
    Over distant towers ;
Paper-made, red, blue an' white,
    All my fav'rite colours.[1]

As up an' up an' up you mount
    On your way to heaven,
Thoughts come, which I cannot count,
    Of the times I've striven

Just to soar away like you,
    Rising to a happier sphere
Deep within yon skies of blue,
    Far from all de strife an' care.

You have got you' singer[2] on,
    Let me hear your singing,
Hear you' pleasant bee-like tone
    On de breezes ringing.

[1] The *l* is swallowed, and the rhyme is good.
[2] A strip of paper shaped like a half moon, and stretched on a thread·
running from one top corner of the kite to the other.

Wider dash your streamin' tail,
  Keep it still a-dancin' !
As across de ditch you sail,
  By the tree-tops glancin'.

Messengers[1] I send along,
  Lee round papers of bright red ;
Up they go to swell you' song,
  Climbin' on the slimber[2] t'read.

Higher fly, my pretty kite,
  Higher, ever higher ;
Draw me with you to your height
  Out the earthly mire.

[1] Round slips of paper, which go twirling up the kite-string.
[2] Slender.

IONE

SAY if you lub me, do tell me truly,
        Ione, Ione ;
For, O me dearie, not'in' can part we,
        Ione, Ione.

Under de bamboo, where de fox-tail [1] grew,
        Ione, Ione,
While de cool breeze blew—sweet, I did pledge
   you,
        Ione, Ione.

Where calalu [2] grows, an' yonder brook flows,
        Ione, Ione,
I held a dog-rose under your li'l [3] nose,
        Ione, Ione.

There where de lee stream plays wid de sunbeam,
        Ione, Ione,
True be'n de love-gleam as a sweet day-dream,
        Ione, Ione.

[1] A grass with heavy plumes.
[2] Spinach, but not the English kind.   [3] Little.

Watchin' de bucktoe [1] under de shadow,
> Ione, Ione,
Of a pear-tree low dat in de stream grow,
> Ione, Ione,

Mek me t'ink how when we were lee children,
> Ione, Ione,
We used to fishen [2] in old Carew Pen, [3]
> Ione, Ione.

Like tiny meshes, curl your black tresses,
> Ione, Ione,
An' my caresses tek widout blushes,
> Ione, Ione.

Kiss me, my airy winsome lee fairy,
> Ione, Ione ;
Are you now weary, little canary,
> Ione, Ione?

Then we will go, pet, as it is sunset,
> Ione, Ione ;
Tek dis sweet vi'let, we will be one yet,
> Ione, Ione.

[1] Small crawfish. [2] Fish.
[3] The Jamaican equivalent for ranche.

KILLIN' NANNY

Two little pickny is watchin',
  While a goat is led to deat';
Dey are little ones of two years,
  An' know naught of badness yet.

De goat is bawlin' fe mussy,[1]
  An' de children watch de sight
As de butcher re'ch[2] his sharp knife,
  An' 'tab[3] wid all his might.

Dey see de red blood flowin';
  An' one chil' trimble an' hide
His face in de mudder's bosom,
  While t'udder look on wide-eyed.

De tears is fallin' down hotly
  From him on de mudder's knee;
De udder wid joy is starin',
  An' clappin' his han's wid glee.

When dey had forgotten Nanny,
  Grown men I see dem again;
An' de forehead of de laugher
  Was brand'[4] wid de mark of Cain.

[1] Mercy.   [2] Reaches, lays hold of.   [3] Stabs.
[4] Branded.

83

MY NATIVE LAND, MY HOME

DERE is no land dat can compare
  Wid you where'er I roam ;
In all de wul' none like you fair,
  My native land, my home.

Jamaica is de nigger's place,
  No mind whe' some declare ;
Although dem call we " no-land race,"
  I know we home is here.

You give me life an' nourishment,
  No udder land I know ;
My lub I neber can repent,
  For all to you I owe.

E'en ef you mek me beggar die,
  I'll trust you all de same,
An' none de less on you rely,
  Nor saddle you wid blame.

Though you may cas'[1] me from your breas'
  An' trample me to deat',
My heart will trus' you none de less,
  My land I won't feget.

[1] Cast.

84

An' I hope none o' your sons would
    Refuse deir strengt' to lend,
An' drain de last drop o' deir blood
    Their country to defend.

You draw de t'ousan' from deir shore,
    An' all 'long keep dem please' ; [1]
De invalid come here fe cure,
    You heal all deir disease.

Your fertile soil grow all o' t'ings [2]
    To full de naygur's wants,
'Tis seamed wid neber-failing springs [3]
    To give dew to de plants. [4]

You hab all t'ings fe mek life bles',
    But buccra 'poil de whole
Wid gove'mint [5] an' all de res',
    Fe worry naygur soul.

Still all dem little chupidness [6]
    Caan' tek away me lub ;
De time when I'll tu'n 'gains' you is
    When you can't give me grub.

[1] And keep them amused and happy all along (all the time of their stay).
[2] All of (the) things.   [3] Brooks.
[4] The dew falls heavily in the valley-bottoms.   [5] Government.
[6] Those little stupidnesses.

TWO-AN'-SIX

MERRY voices chatterin',
Nimble feet dem patterin',
Big an' little, faces gay,
Happy day dis market day.

Sateday ! [1] de marnin' break,
Soon, soon market-people wake ;
An' de light shine from de moon
While dem boy, wid pantaloon
Roll up ober dem knee-pan,
'Tep [2] across de buccra lan'
To de pastur whe' de harse [3]
Feed along wid de jackass,
An' de mule cant' in de track [4]
Wid him tail up in him back,
All de ketchin' to defy,
No ca' how [5] dem boy might try.

In de early marnin'-tide,
When de cocks crow on de hill
An' de stars are shinin' still,
Mirrie by de fireside

[1] Saturday.　　[2] Step.　　[3] Where the horse.
[4] Canters in the track. A Jamaican pasture is seamed with tracks
made by the animals in walking.
[5] I don't care how ; no matter how.

86

Hots[1] de coffee for de lads
Comin' ridin' on de pads
T'rown across dem animul—
Donkey, harse too, an' de mule,
Which at last had come do'n cool.[2]
On de bit dem hol' dem full :
Racin' ober pastur' lan',
See dem comin' ebery man,
Comin' fe de steamin' tea[3]
Ober hilly track an' lea.

Hard-wuk'd donkey on de road
Trottin' wid him ushal[4] load,—
Hamper[5] pack' wi' yam an' grain,
Sour-sop,[6] an' Gub'nor cane.[7]

Cous' Sun[8] sits in hired dray,
Drivin' 'long de market way ;
Whole week grindin' sugar-cane
T'rough de boilin' sun an' rain,
Now, a'ter[9] de toilin' hard,
He goes seekin' his reward,
While he's thinkin' in him min'
Of de dear ones lef' behin',
Of de loved though ailin' wife,
Darlin' treasure of his life,
An' de picknies, six in all,
Whose 'nuff[10] burdens 'pon him fall :

---

[1] Warms.   [2] Given up his skittishness.
[3] Generic name for any non-alcoholic hot drink.
[4] Usual, pronounced without the second *u*.   [5] Panniers.
[6] *Anona muricata*—a fruit.
[7] Governor cane ; a yellow-striped sugar-cane.
[8] Cousin James.   Sun is the regular nickname for James.
[9] After.   [10] Enough=many.

Seben [1] lovin' ones in need,
Seben hungry mouths fe feed ;
On deir wants he thinks alone,
Neber dreamin' of his own,
But gwin' on wid joyful face
Till him re'ch [2] de market-place.

Sugar bears no price te-day,
Though it is de mont' o' May,
When de time is hellish hot,
An' de water-cocoanut [3]
An' de cane bebridge [4] is nice,
Mix' up wid a lilly ice. [5]
Big an' little, great an' small,
Afou yam is all de call ; [6]
Sugar tup an' gill [7] a quart,
Yet de people hab de heart
Wantin' brater [8] top o' i',
Want de sweatin' higgler fe
Ram de pan an' pile i' up,
Yet sell i' fe so-so tup. [9]

Cousin Sun is lookin' sad,
As de market is so bad ;
'Pon him han' him res' him chin,
Quietly sit do'n thinkin'

---

[1] Seven.   [2] Till he reaches.
[3] Immature cocoanut, the milk of which is a delicious drink.
[4] Beverage.   [5] Mixed up with a little ice.
[6] The variety of yam called "ahfoo" is the thing principally asked
for by young and old.
[7] Tup (twopence of the old Jamaica coinage) is 1½d : gill, ¾d.
So "tup and gill" is 2¼d.
[8] Insist on having *brahter*, a little extra on top of (over) the quart.
[9] Sell it for a bare tup.

Of de loved wife sick in bed,
An' de children to be fed—
What de labourers would say
When dem know him couldn' pay;
Also what about de mill
Whe' him hire [1] from ole Bill;
So him think, an' think on so,
Till him t'oughts no more could go.

Then he got up an' began
Pickin' up him sugar-pan: [2]
In his ears rang t'rough de din
"Only two-an'-six a tin!"
What a tale he'd got to tell,
How bad, bad de sugar sell!

Tekin' out de lee amount,
Him set do'n an' begin count;
All de time him min' deh doubt [3]
How expenses would pay out;
Ah, it gnawed him like de ticks,
Sugar sell fe two-an'-six!

So he journeys on de way,
Feelin' sad dis market day;
No e'en buy [4] a little cake
To gi'e baby when she wake,—
Passin' 'long de candy-shop
'Douten eben mek a stop
To buy drops fe las'y [5] son,
For de lilly cash nea' done.

---

[1] Which he hires, or hired.   [2] His sugar pans (tins).
[3] His mind is doubting.   [4] Doesn't even buy.
[5] Lasty (lahsty), pet name for the Benjamin of a family.

So him re'ch him own a groun',
An' de children scamper roun',
Each one stretchin' out him han',
Lookin' to de poor sad man.

Oh, how much he felt de blow,
As he watched dem face fall low,
When dem wait an' nuttin' came
An' drew back deir han's wid shame !
But de sick wife kissed his brow :
"Sun, don't get down-hearted now ;
Ef we only pay expense
We mus' wuk we common-sense,
Cut an' carve, an' carve an' cut,
Mek gill sarbe fe quattiewut' ; [1]
We mus' try mek two ends meet
Neber mind how hard be it.
We won't mind de haul an' pull,
While dem pickny belly full." [2]

An' de shadow lef' him face,
An' him felt an inward peace,
As he blessed his better part
For her sweet an' gentle heart :
"Dear one o' my heart, my breat',
Won't I lub you to de deat'?
When my heart is weak an' sad,
Who but you can mek it glad ?"

So dey kissed an' kissed again,
An' deir t'oughts were not on pain,
But was 'way down in de sout'
Where dey'd wedded in deir yout',

---

[1] Make ¾d. serve for quattieworth, 1½d.
[2] If only the children have enough to eat.

In de marnin' of deir life
Free from all de grief an' strife,
Happy in de marnin' light,
Never thinkin' of de night.

So dey k'lated [1] eberyt'ing ;
An' de profit it could bring,
A'ter all de business fix', [2]
Was a princely two-an'-six.

[1] Calculated.
[2] After all the business was fixed, *i.e.*, when the accounts were made up.

COMPENSATION

DERE is a rest-place for de weary feet,
An' for de bitter cup a conquering sweet:
For sore an' burdened hearts dere'll be a balm,
And after days of tempest comes a calm.

For every smallest wrong dere is a right,
An' t'rough de dark shall gleam a ray of light:
Oppression for a season may endure,
But 'tis true wud, " For ebery ill a cure."

Den let me not t'ink hard of those who use
Deir power tyrannously an' abuse:
Let me remember always while I live,
De noblest of all deeds is to forgive.

This, not revenge, is sweet: this lifs[1] de soul
An' meks it wort' while[2] in a empty wul':
Far better than an old an' outworn creed
'Tis each day to do one such noble deed.

[1] Lifts.   [2] Something worth.

HEARTLESS RHODA

Kiss me, as you want it so;
    Lub me, ef it wort' de while; [1]
Yet I feel it an' I know [2]
Dat, as t'rough de wul' you go,
    You will oft look back an' smile
At de t'ings which you now do.

Tek me to de church te-day,
    Call me wife as you go home;
Hard fate, smilin' at us, say [3]
Dat de whole is so-so play;
    Soon de ushal en' will come,
An' we both will choice [4] our way.

*   *   *   *   *   *   *

Spare you' breat', me husban' true,
    I be'n marry you fe fun: [5]
Lub dat las' long is a few, [6]
An' I hadn' much fe you.
    I be'n tell you it would done, [7]
All whe' come is wha' you do. [8]

[1] Love me, if it is worth while, *i.e.* if you think it worth while.
[2] Yet I feel and know.   [3] Says.
[4] Choose, *i.e,* go our several ways.
[5] I married you with no serious purpose.   [6] Seldom met with.
[7] I did tell (told) you it would soon come to an end.
[8] All that has happened is your doing.

Life I only care to see
    In de way dat udders[1] live ;
I experiment to be
All dat fate can mek o' me :
    Glad I tek all whe' she give,
For I'm hopin' to be free. [2]

[1] Others.

[2] A free paraphrase will best explain the meaning of these six lines. Rhoda sees other girls marry, and out of pure curiosity she wants to find out what married life is like. So she makes the experiment,—though this [marriage] is only one of the things that Fate has in store for her. And she takes gladly whatever Fate gives, always hoping (and meaning) to change the present experience for another.

A DREAM

THE roosters give the signal for daybreak,
   And through my window[1] pours the grey of
     morn ;
Refreshing breezes fan me as I wake,
   And down the valley sounds the wesly[2] horn.

Day broadens, and I ope the window wide,[3]
   And brilliant sunbeams, mixing, rush between
The gaping blinds, while down at my bedside
   I kneel to utter praise to the Unseen.

The torch-light glistens through the wattle-pane,[4]
   And clouds of smoke wreathe upward to the
     skies ;
My brother at the squeezer juices cane,[5]
   And visions of tea-hour before me rise.

---

[1] The window is a jalousie, and its blinds (slats) are shut.
[2] Word of uncertain origin. The wesly horn sounds when any work
in common is to be undertaken.
[3] Throw the slats into a horizontal position.
[4] The bedroom is separated from the kitchen by panes of undaubed
wattle, through which is seen the glimmer of the burning torch-wood.
[5] At the squeezer (a rough home-made machine) is extracting juice
from sugar-canes.

95

Leaving the valley's cup the fleeting fog
　　Steals up the hill-sides decked with sunbeams
　　　　rare,
Which send their search-rays 'neath the time-worn
　　　　log,
　　And drive the sleeping majoes[1] from their lair.

But there are some that yest'reve was the last
　　For them to sleep into their watery bed ;
For now my treacherous fish-pot has them fast,
　　Their cruel foe which they had so long dread'.[2]

Right joyfully I hear the school-bell ring,
　　And by my sister's side away I trot ;
I'm happy as the swee-swees[3] on the wing,
　　And feel naught but contentment in my lot.

I lightly gambol on the school-yard green,
　　And where the damsels[4] by the bamboo grove
In beautiful and stately growth are seen,
　　For tiny shiny star-apples I rove.

　　　*　　　*　　　*　　　*　　　*　　　*

The morning wind blows softly past my door,
　　And we prepare for work with gladsome heart ;
Sweetly the wesly horn resounds once more,
　　　A warning that 'tis time for us to start.

---

[1] Pronounce the *ma* as in French —fresh-water shrimps, which live in the hill-side brooklets.
[2] Whom for so long a time they had dreaded.
[3] Quits. The name imitates their chirping song.
[4] The damsel (corruption of damson, probably) is like a small star-apple.

I scamper quickly 'cross the fire-burnt soil,·
  And the coarse grass-tufts prick my tender feet ;
I watch my father at his honest toil,
  And wonder how he stands the sun's fierce heat.

A winding footpath down the woodland leads,
  And through the tall fox-tails I wend my way
Down to the brooklet where the pea-dove feeds,
  And bucktoes[1] in the water are at play.

And watching as the bubbles rise and fall,
  I hear above the murmur of the dale
The tropic music dear to great and small,
  The joyous outburst of the nightingale.

*   *   *   *   *   *

Gone now those happy days when all was blest,
  For I have left my home and kindred dear ;
In a strange place I am a stranger's guest,
  The pains, the real in life, I've now to bear.

No more again I'll idle at my will,
  Running the mongoose down upon the lea ;
No more I'll jostle[2] Monty up the hill,
  To pick the cashews[3] off the laden tree.

I feel the sweetness of those days again,
  And hate, so hate, on the past scenes to look ;
All night in dreaming comes the awful pain,
  All day I groan beneath the iron yoke.

---

[1] Small crawfish.
[2] Race and foul.   [3] A fruit (*Anacardium occidentale*).

In mercy then, ye Gods, deal me swift death !
   Ah ! you refuse, and life instead you give ;
You keep me here and still prolong my breath,
   That I may suffer all the days I live.

     *   *   *   *   *   *

'Tis home again, but not the home of yore ;
   Sadly the scenes of bygone days I view,
And as I walk the olden paths once more,
   My heart grows chilly as the morning dew.

But see ! to-day again my life is glad,
   My heart no more is lone, nor will it pine ;
A comfort comes, an earthly fairy clad
   In white, who guides me with her hand in mine.

Her lustrous eyes gleam only tender love,
   And viewing her, an angel form I see ;
I feed my spirit on my gentle dove,
   My sweetheart Lee, my darling Idalee.[1]

And where the peenies glow with greenish fire,
   We kiss and kiss and pledge our hearts as true ;
Of sweet love-words and hugs we never tire,
   But felt more sorry that they were so few.

     *   *   *   *   *   *

[1] This tacking of a syllable on to well-known names is common in Jamaica.

I leave my home again, wand'ring afar,
   But goes with me her true, her gentle heart,
Ever to be my hope, my guiding star,
   And whisperings of comfort to impart.

Methinks we're strolling by the woodland stream,
   And my frame thrills with joy to hear her sing:
But, O my God! 'tis all—'tis all a dream;
   This is the end, the rude awakening.

RISE AND FALL

[Thoughts of Burns—with apologies to his immortal spirit for making him speak in Jamaica dialect.]

DEY read[1] 'em again an' again,
    An' laugh an' cry[2] at 'em in turn ;
I felt I was gettin' quite vain,
    But dere was a lesson fe learn.

My poverty quickly took wing,
    Of life no experience had I ;
I couldn' then want anyt'ing
    Dat kindness or money could buy.

Dey tek me away from me lan',
    De gay o' de wul' to behold,
An' roam me t'rough palaces gran',
    An' show'red on me honour untold.

I went to de ballroom at night,
    An' danced wid de belles of de hour ;
Half dazed by de glitterin' light,
    I lounged in de palm-covered bower.

[1] Preterite.   [2] Laughed and cried.

I flirted wid beautiful girls,
　An' drank o' de wine flowin' red ;
I felt my brain movin' in whirls,
　An' knew I was losin' my head.

But soon I was tired of it all,
　My spirit was weary to roam ; [1]
De life grew as bitter as gall,
　I hungered again for my home.

Te-day I am back in me lan',
　Forgotten by all de gay throng,
A poorer but far wiser man,
　An' knowin' de right from de wrong.

[1] Sick of roaming.

BENEATH THE YAMPY[1] SHADE

WE sit beneat' de yampy shade,
  My lee sweetheart an' I ;
De gully[2] ripples 'cross de glade,
  Tom Rafflins[3] hurry by.

Her pa an' ma about de fiel'
  Are brukin'[4] sugar-pine ;
An' plenty, plenty is de yiel',
  Dem look so pink[5] an' fine.

We listen to a rapturous chune[6]
  Outpourin' from above ;
De swee-swees,[7] blithesome birds of June,
  They sing to us of love.

She plays wid de triangle leaves,
  Her hand within mine slips ;
She murmurs love, her bosom heaves,
  I kiss her ripe, ripe lips.

[1] The Yampy, or Indian Yam, has very beautiful triangular leaves. Yams of all kinds climb, like hops, on sticks or trees.
[2] Brook. The word is more generally used in the sense of *precipice*.
[3] Mad ants, which run very quickly.
[4] Breaking. Pine-apples are gathered by bending down the stalk, which snaps cleanly off.
[5] Choice, nice. *Cf.* the phrase, l'ink of perfection.
[6] Tune.　　　　　[7] Quits.

De cockstones[1] raise deir droopin' heads
    To view her pretty feet ;
De skellions[2] trimble in deir beds,
    Dey grudge our lub so sweet—

Love sweeter than a bridal dream,
    A mudder's fondest kiss ;
Love purer than a crystal stream,
    De height of eart'ly bliss.

We hear again de swee-swees' song
    Outpourin' on de air ;
Dey sing for yout', an' we are young
    An' know naught 'bouten care.

We sit beneat' de yampy shade,
    We pledge our hearts anew ;
De swee-swees droop, de bell-flowers[3] fade
    Before our love so true.

[1] Red peas, French beans.
[2] Scallions—a non-bulbing onion.
[3] *Datura suaveolens*, whose great white trumpets flag as the sun gets hot.

TO INSPECTOR W. E. CLARK

(ON THE EVE OF HIS DEPARTURE FOR ENGLAND)

FAREWELL, dear Sir, a sad farewell !
An' as across the deep you sail,
   Bon voyage we wish you :
We love you deepest as we can,[1]
As officer an' gentleman,
   With love sincere an' true.

Though often you have been our judge,
We never owed you one lee grudge,
   For you were always fair :
So, as the sad farewell we say,
May Neptune guide you, Sir, we pray,
   With ever watchful care.

But as you travel to our home,[2]
Sad are the strange thoughts which *will* come,
   Bringin' an aching pain ;
That as this is a fitful life,
With disappointments ever rife,
   We may not meet again.

---

[1] With all our heart.   [2] England.

Yet while our hearts are filled with grief,
The god of hope brings sweet relief
   An' bids us not despair :
Of all our thoughts we cannot tell,
But wish you, Sir, a fond farewell,
   A farewell of good cheer.

21st May, 1911.

TO CLARENDON HILLS AND H. A. H.

Loved Clarendon hills,
Dear Clarendon hills,
Oh! I feel de chills,
Yes, I feel de chills
Coursin' t'rough me frame
When I call your name,[1]
Dear Clarendon hills,
Loved Clarendon hills.

Wand'rin', wand'rin' far,
Weary, wan'drin' far
'Douten guidin' star,
Not a guidin' star,
Still my love's for you
Ever, ever true,
Though I wander far,
Weary wander far.

H. A. H., my frien',
Ever cherished frien',
I'll return again,
Yes, return again :
Think, O think of me
Tossed on life's dark sea,
H. A. H., my frien',
Dearest, fondest frien'.

[1] Speak of you.

106

Ah, dear frien' o' mine,
Love me, frien' o' mine,
Wid that love of thine
Passin' love of womenkin',[1]
More dan love of womenkin' :
Clasp me to your breast,
Pillow me to rest,
Fait'ful frien' o' mine,
Truest frien' o' mine.

Though you may be sad,
Sorrowin' an' sad,
Never min' dat, lad,
Don't you min' dat, lad !
Live, O live your life,
Trample on de strife,
Though you may be sad,
Always, always sad.

Loved Clarendon hills,
Cherished frien' o' mine,
Oh, my bosom thrills,
Soul an' body pine :
T'rough de wul' I rove,
Pinin' for your love,
Blest Clarendon hills,
Dearest frien' o' mine.

[1] 2 Sam. i. 26.

WHEN YOU WANT A BELLYFUL

When you want a bellyful,
   Tearin' piece o' one,[1]
Mek up fire, wash you' pot,
   Full i' wid cockstone.

Nuttin' good as cockstone soup
   For a bellyful ;
Only, when you use i' hot,
   You can sweat no bull.[2]

An' to mek you know de trut',
   Dere's anedder flaw ;
Ef you use too much o' i',
   It wi' paunch you' maw.[3]

---

[1] This whole line is a single intensifying adjective ; and the two lines together are equivalent to "When you want a tremendous bellyful."

[2] It makes you sweat like a ('no'— pronounced very short in this sense) bull.

[3] Make your belly swell.

108

Growin' wid de fat blue corn,
　　Pretty cockstone peas—
Lilly blossom, vi'let-like,[1]
　　Drawin' wuker bees—

We look on dem growin' dere,
　　Pokin' up dem head,
Lilly, lilly, t'rough de corn,
　　Till de pod dem shed.[2]

An' we watch de all-green pods
　　Stripin' bit by bit ;
Green leaves gettin' yellow coat,
　　Showin dey were fit.[3]

So we went an' pull dem up,[4]
　　Reaped a goodly lot,
Shell some o' de pinkish grain,
　　Put dem in a pot.[5]

But I tell you, Sir, again,
　　Cockstone soup no good ;[6]
From experience I t'ink
　　'Tis de wus' o' food.[7]

---

[1] Violet coloured.　　　　　[2] Until the pods are formed.
[3] Showing that the peas were fit to pick.
[4] These red peas are pulled up by the roots.
[5] In the pot.　　[6] Is not good.　　[7] The worst of foods.

When de reapin'-time come roun',
  I dry fe me part ; [1]
Sellin' i', when it get scarce,
  For a bob a quart. [2]

When you need a bellyful,
  Gripin' piece o' one,
Shub up fire under pot,
  Put in dry cockstone.

[1] I dry my share.
[2] The usual price is ' bit,' *i.e.*, 4½d.

STROKES OF THE TAMARIND
SWITCH

I DARED not look at him,
My eyes with tears were dim,
   My spirit filled with hate
      Of man's depravity,
   I hurried through the gate.

I went but I returned,
While in my bosom burned
   The monstrous wrong that we
      Oft bring upon ourselves,
   And yet we cannot see.

Poor little erring wretch!
The cutting tamarind switch
   Had left its bloody mark,
      And on his legs were streaks
   That looked like boiling bark.[1]

[1] Floors are dyed with a blood-red decoction made from the bark of trees.

III

I spoke to him the while :
At first he tried to smile,
   But the long pent-up tears
     Came gushing in a flood ;
   He was but of tender years.

With eyes bloodshot and red,
He told me of a father dead
   And lads like himself rude,
     Who goaded him to wrong :
   He for the future promised to be good.

The mother yesterday
Said she was sending him away,
   Away across the seas :
     She told of futile prayers
   Said on her wearied knees.

I wished the lad good-bye,
And left him with a sigh :
   Again I heard him talk—
     His limbs, he said, were sore,
   He could not walk.

I 'member when a smaller boy,
A mother's pride, a mother's joy,
   I too was very rude :
     They beat me too, though not the same,[1]
   And has it done me good ?

[1] Not so severely.

NOTE BY THE AUTHOR.—This was a lad of fifteen. No doubt he deserved the flogging administered by order of the Court : still, I could not bear to see him—my own flesh—stretched out over the bench, so I went away to the Post Office near by. When I returned, all was over. I saw his naked bleeding form, and through the terrible ordeal—so they told me—he never cried. But when I spoke to him he broke down, told me between his bursts of tears how he had been led astray by bad companions, and that his mother intended sending him over-sea. He could scarcely walk, so I gave him tickets for the tram. He had a trustful face. A few minutes after, my bitterness of spirit at the miserable necessity of such punishment came forth in song, which I leave rugged and unpolished as I wrote it at the moment.

MY PRETTY DAN

I HAVE a póliceman down at de Bay,[1]
An' he is true to me though far away.

I love my pólice, and he loves me too,
An' he has promised he'll be ever true.

My little bobby is a darlin' one,
An' he's de prettiest you could set eyes 'pon.

When he be'n station' up de countryside,
Fus' time I shun him sake o' foolish pride.

But as I watched him patrolling his beat,
I got to find out he was nice an' neat.

More still I foun' out he was extra kin',
An' dat his precious heart was wholly mine.

Den I became his own a true sweetheart,
An' while life last we're hopin' not fe part.

---

[1] Morant Bay and similarly named seaside towns are always called simply 'the Bay' by the people of the district.

114

He wears a truncheon an' a handcuff case,
An' pretty cap to match his pretty face.

Dear lilly p'liceman stationed down de sout',
I feel your kisses rainin' on my mout'.

I could not give against [1] a póliceman;
For if I do, how could I lub my Dan?

Prettiest of naygur is my dear police,
We'll lub foreber, an' our lub won't cease.

I have a póliceman down at de Bay,
An' he is true to me though far away.

[1] Revile, abuse, vilify.

RIBBER COME-DO'N[1]

FROM de top o' Clarendon hill
  Chock down to Clarendon plain
De ribber is rushin' an' tearin'
  'Count o' de showers o' rain.

An' a mudder, anxious an' sad,
  Two whole days be'n gone away,
A-buyin' fresh fish fe tu'n han'[2]
  Slap do'n at Old Harbour Bay.

But de dark ribber kept her back,
  Dat night she couldn' get home,
While a six-week-old baby wailed,
  An' wailed for a mudder to come.

An' a fader too was away
  'Cross de Minha[3] wukin' him groun',[4]
So him couldn' get home dat night
  Sake o' de ribber come-do'n.

[1] The river in flood.   [2] To peddle.
[3] The Rio Minho : pronounce 'miner.'
[4] Cultivating his ground or provision-field.

116

Dere were four udder little ones
   'Sides de babe of six weeks old,
An' dey cried an' looked to no use,[1]
   An' oh dey were hungry an' cold !

So de lee fourteen-year-old gal,
   De eldest one o' de lot,
Was sad as she knelt by the babe
   An' byaed [2] her on de cot.

      " Bya, bya, me baby,
        Baby want go sleepy."

She look 'pon de Manchinic [3] tree,
   Not a piece of mancha fe eat ;
De Jack-fruit dem bear well anuff,
   But dere wasn't one o' dem fit.[4]

Nor puppa nor mumma could come,
   Aldough it be'n now nightfall ;
De rain pour do'n an' de wind blow,
   An' de picknanies dem still bawl.

So de poo' Milly 'tarted out
   To whe' a kin' neighbour lib,
Fe see ef a bite o' nenyam [5]
   Dem couldn' p'raps manage fe gib.

---

[1] In vain.   [2] A verb formed from hushaby.
[3] Martinique, the best variety of Banana. Hence mancha for banana.
[4] Ripe.   [5] Food.

"Ebenin', cousin Anna,
Me deh beg you couple banna,[1]
For dem tarra one[2] is berry hungry home;
We puppa ober May,[3] ma,
We mumma gone a Bay, ma,
An' we caan' tell warra[4] time dem gwin' go
    come."

The kind district mother thought
    Of her own boy far away,
An' wondered much how he fared
    In a foreign land that day.

She opened de cupboard door
    An' took from it warra be'n sabe,
A few bits o' yam an' lee meal,
    An' a pint o' milk fe de babe.

De parents dat night couldn' come,
    De howlin' wind didn' lull,
But de picknanies went to bed
    Wid a nuff nuff bellyful.

[1] I am begging a few bananas of you.
[2] Those other ones, *i.e.*, the little children at home.
[3] Over at Mayfield.   [4] What.

A COUNTRY GIRL

"Lelia gal, why in this town do you stay?
Why, tell me, why did you wander away?
Why will you aimlessly foolishly roam,
Won't you come back to your old country home?"

"Country life, Fed, has no pleasures for me,
I wanted de gay o' de city to see,
To wear ebery Sunday a prettier gown,
Da's why I came to de beautiful town."

"Well, have you gotten de joys dat you sought?
If so, were not all o' dem too dearly bought?
Yes, Liel, you do wear a prettier dress,
But have you not suffered, my girl, more or less?

"Hold up your head! look not down, tell me truth,
Have you not bartered your innocent youth?
Are you de Lelia, true Lelia, of old,
Or have you swopped out your honour for gold?"

"Fed, it was horrid de lone country life!
I suffered—for sometimes e'en hunger was rife;
An' when I came, Fed, to try my chance here,
I thought there would be no more troubles to bear.

119

" But troubles there were an' in plenty, my lad,
Oh, dey were bitter, an' oh, I was sad !
Weary an' baffled an' hungry an' lone,
I gave up my spirit to sigh an' to moan.

" After dat ?—O, Feddy, press me not so :
De truth ?—well, I sank to de lowest of de low ;
I gave up all honour, I took a new name
An' tried to be happy, deep sunk in de shame.

" Dere was no other way, Fed, I could live,
Dat was de gift dat a gay town could give ;
I tried to be glad in de open daylight,
But sorrowed an' moaned in de deep o' de night.

" No, Fed, I never could go home again :
' Worse than I left it ?' ah, there was de pain,
To meet up wid some o' my former schoolmates
An' listen to all o' deir taunts an' deir hates.

" Dere now, you bound me to tell you o' all,
Of all de sad suff'rings dat led to my fall ;
I'm gone past reclaiming, so what must I do
But live de bad life an' mek de good go ?"

" Lelia, I want you to come out de sin,
Come home an' try a new life fe begin ;
Mek up you min', gal, fe wuk wid you' han',
Plant peas an' corn in de fat country lan'.

" Dere is no life, gal, so pleasant, so good,
Contented and happy you'll eat your lee food ;
No one at home know 'bout wha' you've jes' said,
So, Liel, of exposure you needn't be 'fraid."

"Don't t'ink I care 'bout exposure, my boy !
 Dat which you call sin is now fe me joy ;
 Country for Lelia will have no more charm,
 I'll live on de same way, 'twill do me no harm.

" And after all, many gals richer than me,
 Pretty white girlies of better degree,
 Live as I do, an' are happy an' gay,
 Then why should not I be as happy as they ?"

MY SOLDIER-LAD

SEE yonder soldier-lad
In Zouave jacket clad?
   His lovin' heart is mine,
His heart so bright an' glad ;
   My soul an' spirit combine
To love my soldier-lad.

      O my dear lilly soldier-lad,
         I am true an' so are you ;
      And oh, my lovin' heart is glad,
         For I know that you are true.

My pretty soldier-boy,
He is my only joy :
   He loves me with his might,
A love without alloy,
   My one, my true delight,
My pretty soldier-boy.

      O my dear lilly soldier-lad, etc.

My own lee soldier true,
He is a bandsman too ;
   An' when he's in the stand,
His sweet eyes playin' blue,
   He carries off the band,
My handsome soldier true.

      O my dear lilly soldier-lad, etc.

My precious lilly pet,
He plays a clarinet :
  De gals dem envy me,
But him they cannot get ;
  Dem hate we both to see,
Me an' my precious pet.

  O my dear lilly soldier-lad, etc.

Where coolin' breezes blow,
An' silvery gullies flow
  Do'n t'rough de bamboo grove,
The amorous pea-doves coo :
  They're cooin' of my love,
While freshenin' breezes blow.

  O my dear lilly soldier-lad, etc.

My dear Bermudan lad
In baggy trousies clad,
  I love you wid whole heart,
A heart that's true an' glad ;
  Our love can never part,
My darlin' bandsy lad.

  O my dear lilly soldier-lad, etc.

MY MOUNTAIN HOME

DE mango tree in yellow bloom,
  De pretty akee seed,
De mammee where de John-to-whits [1] come
  To have their daily feed,

Show you de place where I was born,
  Of which I am so proud,
'Mongst de banana-field an' corn
  On a lone mountain-road.

One Sunday marnin' 'fo' de hour
  Fe service-time come on,
Ma say dat I be'n born to her
  Her little las'y [2] son.

Those early days be'n neber dull,
  My heart was ebergreen ;
How I did lub my little wul'
  Surrounded by pingwin ! [3]

An' growin' up, with sweet freedom
  About de yard I'd run ;
An' tired out I'd hide me from
  De fierce heat of de sun.

[1] Pronounce in two syllables.   [2] Lasty, diminutive of "last."
[3] The wild pineapple (*Bromelia Pinguin*).

124

So glad I was de fus' day when
  Ma sent me to de spring;
I was so happy feelin' then
  Dat I could do somet'ing.

De early days pass quickly 'long,
  Soon I became a man,
An' one day found myself among
  Strange folks in a strange lan'.

My little joys, my wholesome min',
  Dey bullied out o' me,
And made me daily mourn an' pine
  An' wish dat I was free.

Dey taught me to distrust my life,
  Dey taught me what was grief;
For months I travailed in de strife,
  'Fo' I could find relief.

But I'll return again, my Will,
  An' where my wild ferns grow
An' weep for me on Dawkin's Hill,
  Dere, Willie, I shall go.

An' dere is somet'ing near forgot,
  Although I lub it best;
It is de loved, de hallowed spot
  Where my dear mother rest.

Look good [1] an' find it, Willie dear,
  See dat from bush 'tis free ;
Remember that my heart is near,
  An' you say you lub me.

An' plant on it my fav'rite fern,
  Which I be'n usual wear ;
In days to come I shall return
  To end my wand'rin's dere.

[1] Carefully.

TO BENNIE

(IN ANSWER TO A LETTER)

YOU say, dearest comrade, my love has grown
    cold,
But you are mistaken, it burns as of old ;
And no power below, dearest lad, nor above,
Can ever lessen, frien' Bennie, my love.

Could you but look in my eyes, you would see
That 'tis a wrong thought you have about me ;
Could you but feel my hand laid on your head,
Never again would you say what you've said.

Naught, O my Bennie, our friendship can sever,
Dearly I love you, shall love you for ever ;
Moment by moment my thoughts are of you,
Trust me, oh, trust me, for aye to be true.

HOPPING OFF THE TRAM

It would not stop,
So I took a hop,
An', Lard oh, my foot a miss ![1]
It sent me do'n
Slam on de groun',
An' I had a dusty kiss.

The car went 'long
With its hummin' song,
An' I too went my way ;
But the sudden fall
I did recall,
And shall for many a day.

[1] Tripped.

TO A COMRADE[1]

LITTLE comrade, never min'
Though another is unkin';
"Of de pain o' dis ya wul'
We must suck we bellyful."[2]

Little comrade, moan not so,
Oh, you fill my heart with woe !
Sad I listen to your cries,
Can't you ope your burnin' eyes?

Little comrade, though 'tis hot,[3]
Say you will revenge him not :[4]
Talk not thus, you mek me grieve,
Promise me you will forgive.

Little comrade, never min'
Though a brother is unkin';
Treat him kindest as you can,
Show yourself the better man.

[1] A corrosive fluid had been wilfully thrown in his face. —*Au.*
[2] See *Whe' fe do*, which the author and his little comrade had been
reading together.
[3] Painful.   [4] Tell me you will not take vengeance on him.

JUBBA[1]

My Jubba waiting dere fe me ;
Me, knowin', went out on de spree,
An' she, she wait deh till midnight,
Bleach-bleachin' in de cold moonlight :
An' when at last I did go home
I found out dat she had just come,
An' now she tu'n her back away,
An' won't listen a wud I say.

   Forgive me, Jubba, Jubba dear,
   As you are standing, standing there,
   An' I will no more mek you grieve,
   My Jubba, ef you'll but forgive.

I'll go to no more dancing booth,
I'll play no more wid flirty Ruth,
I didn' mean a t'ing, Jubba,
I didn' know you'd bex fe da' ;
I only took two set o' dance
An' at de bidding[2] tried me chance ;
I buy de big crown-bread fe you,
An' won't you tek it, Jubba?—do.

---

[1] The *u* has the value of the *oo* in *look*.
[2] An auction of loaves of fine bread, profusely decorated by the baker's art, is a feature of rustic dances.

Forgive me, Jubba, Jubba dear, etc.

It was a nice tea-meeting though,
None o' de boy dem wasn' slow,
An' it was pack' wid pretty gal,
So de young man was in dem sall ;[1]
But when I 'member you a yard[2]
I know dat you would t'ink it hard,
Aldough, Jubba, 'twas sake o' spite
Mek say you wouldn' come te-night.[3]

Forgive me, Jubba, Jubba dear, etc.

I lef' you, Jub, in such a state,
I neber knew dat you would wait ;
Yet all de while I couldn' res',
De t'ought o' you was in me breas' ;
So nummo time I couldn' was'e,
But me go get me pillow-case[4]
An' put in deh you bread an' cake—
Forgive me, Jubba, fe God sake !

Forgive me, Jubba, Jubba dear, etc.

[1] So the young men had a fine time of it.
[2] In the yard, *i.e.*, at home.
[3] Out of caprice Jubba had refused to go to the dance : she was jealously watching outside the booth, while her young man imagined she was at home.
[4] The usual receptacle for bread.

APPENDIX OF TUNES

TAKEN ABACK

Andantino.

Let me go, Joe, for I want go home: Can't

stan' wid you, For pa might go come;

An' if him on - ly hab him rum, I

don't know what - e - ber I'll do.

Go wid you, Joe?—you don't lub me den! I

shame o' you—Gals caan' trust you men! An

I be'n tek - in' you fe me frien'; Good-

night, Joe, you've prov-en un - true.

PLEADING

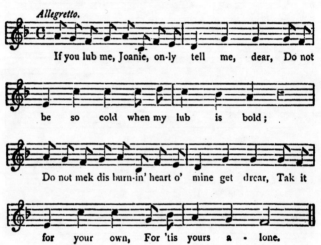

If you lub me, Joanie, on-ly tell me, dear, Do not be so cold when my lub is bold; Do not mek dis burn-in' heart o' mine get drear, Tak it for your own, For 'tis yours a - lone.

IONE

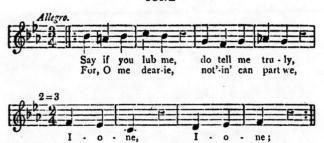

Say if you lub me, do tell me tru - ly,
For, O me dear-ie, not'-in' can part we,

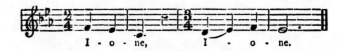

I - o - ne, I - o - ne;

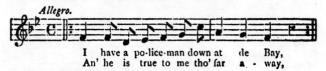

Tek dis sweet vi' - let, we will be one yet,

I - o - ne, I - o - ne.

MY PRETTY DAN

I have a po-lice-man down at de Bay,
An' he is true to me tho' far a - way,

far a - way.

MY SOLDIER LAD

See yonder soldier lad in zouave jac-ket
clad? His lov-in' heart is mine, His heart so bright an'
glad; My soul an' spirit com-bine to love my sol-dier
lad. O my dear lil-ly sol-dier lad,
I am true an' so are you, And oh, my lov-in'
heart is glad— For I know that you are true.

JUBBA.

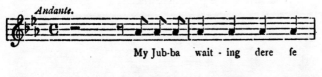

My Jub-ba wait - ing dere fe

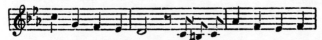

me ; Me, knowin', went out on de spree, An' she, she

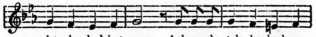

wait deh till mid-night, Bleach-bleachin' in de cold moon-

light : An' when at last I did go home I found out

dat she had just come, An' now she tu'n her back a-

way, An' won't list-en a wud I say. Forgive me

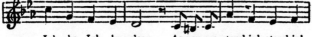

Jub - ba, Jub - ba dear, As you are stand-in', stand-in'

there, An' I will no more mek you grieve, My Jub-ba,

ef you'll but for - give ——, An' I will no more mek you

grieve, My Jub-ba ef you'll but for - give.

CONSTAB BALLADS

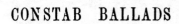

CONSTAB BALLADS

BY

CLAUDE McKAY

Volume II

PREFACE

LET me confess it at once. I had not in me the stuff that goes to the making of a good constable; for I am so constituted that imagination outruns discretion, and it is my misfortune to have a most improper sympathy with wrongdoers. I therefore never "made cases," but turning, like Nelson, a blind eye to what it was my manifest duty to see, tried to make peace, which seemed to me better.

Moreover, I am, by temperament, unadaptive; by which I mean that it is not in me to conform cheerfully to uncongenial usages. We blacks are all somewhat impatient of discipline, and to the natural impatience of my race there was added, in my particular case, a peculiar sensitiveness which made certain forms of discipline irksome, and a fierce hatred of injustice. Not that I ever openly rebelled; but the rebellion was in my heart, and it was fomented by the inevitable rubs of daily life—trifles to most of my comrades, but to me calamities and tragedies. To relieve my feelings, I wrote poems, and into them I poured my heart in its various moods. This volume consists of a selection from these poems.

The life was, as it happened, unsuited to me, and I to

it ; but I do not regret my experiences. If I had enemies whom I hated, I also had close friends whom I loved.

One word in conclusion. As constituted by the authorities the Force is admirable, and it only remains for the men themselves, and especially the sub-officers, to make it what it should be, a harmonious band of brothers.

C. McK.

CONTENTS

10 CONTENTS

DE ROUTE MARCH

In de fus' squad an' de front rank,
'Side me dear Will on de right flank,
From de drill-groun' at the old camp
We went marchin' on a long tramp.

In de forefront was de gay band,
An' de music it was ring grand ;
O how jolly were we boys, oh,
As we marched 'long t'rough St. Jago !

As we tramped on out de dull town,
Keepin' time so[1] to de drum's soun',
All de folkses as dey ran out,
Started dancin' with a glad shout.

We went swingin' do'n de steep hill,
Me so happy by my dear Will,
Wid our carbines slung about we,
An' our glad hearts like de air free.

We drank a draught from a pure brook
Dat came windin' roun' a lee nook ;
Then homeward turned from de cool spring,
Wid our good S. M. commanding.

[1] pointing to the feet.

11

To de music wid a good will
We went tramp-trampin' up de hill,
An' back to camp strode marchin' t'rough
De sad ruins of St. Jago.

FLAT-FOOT DRILL

Fus' beginnin', flat-foot drill,
  Larnin' how fe mek right tu'n :
" 'Tention ! keep you' han's dem still,
Can't you tek in dat a li'l ?
  Hearin' all, but larnin' none.

" But seems unno all do'n-ca',
  Won't mek up you' min' fe larn ;
Drill-instructor boun' fe swea',
Dealin' wid you' class all day,
  Neber see such from A barn.

" Right tu'n, you damn' bungo brut'.!
  Do it *so*, you mountain man ;
Car' behin' de bluff lef' foot,
Seems i' frighten fe de boot !
  Why you won't keep do'n you' han' ?

" Shet you' mout' !   A wan' no chat !
  Fabour say you pick up nong,[1]
Sence you nyamin' Depôt fat
An' 'top sleep 'pon so-so mat,
  But A mean fe pull you' tongue.[2]

---

[1] It seems you are getting " beany " now.
[2] so that you can't talk.

" Wonder when unno wi' fit
  Fe move up in-a fus' squad,
Use carbine an' bayonet !
Wait dough,—unno wi' larn yet,—
  Me wi' drill you ti' you mad."

BENNIE'S DEPARTURE

ALL dat week was cold an' dreary,
　　An' I worked wid heavy heart;
All my limbs were weak an' weary,
　　When I knew that we would part;
An' I thought of our first meeting
　　On dat pleasant day o' June,
Of his kind an' modest greeting
　　When we met dat afternoon;

Of de cáprice o' de weader,
　　How de harsh rain fell dat day,
How we kissed de book togeder,
　　An' our hearts were light an' gay;
How we started homewards drivin',
　　Last civilian drive in train;
How we half-feared de arrivin',
　　Knowin' we were not free again;

How we feared do'n to de layin'
　　By of our loved old-time dress,
An' to each udder kept sayin'
　　All might be unhappiness;
How our lives be'n full o' gladness,
　　Drillin' wid hearts light an' free;
How for days all would be sadness
　　When we quarrelled foolishly.

An' de sad, glad recollection
　　Brought a strange thrill to my soul,
'Memberin' how his affection
　　Gave joy in a barren wul':
As I thought then, my mind goin'
　　Back to mem'ries, oh! so dear,—
As I felt de burden growin',
　　Jes' so shall I write it here.

We were once more on de drill-ground,
　　Me so happy by his side,
One in passion, one in will, bound
　　By a boundless love an' wide:
Daily you would see us drinkin'
　　Our tea by de mess-room door,
Every passin' moment linkin'
　　Us togeder more an' more.

After little lazy leanin',
　　Sittin' on de window-sill,
Me would start our carbine-cleanin'
　　For de eight o'clock big drill:
'Fo' me he be'n always ready,
　　An' as smart as smart could be;
He was always quick, yet steady,
　　Not of wav'rin' min' like me.

When de time was awful dull in
　　De ole borin' Depôt-school,
An' me face was changed an' sullen,
　　An' I kicked against de rule,
He would speak to me so sweetly,
　　Tellin' me to bear my fate,

An' his lovin' words completely
　　Helped me to forget de hate.

An' my heart would start a-pinin'
　　Ef, when one o'clock came roun',
He was not beside me dinin',
　　But be'n at some duty boun':
Not a t'ing could sweet me eatin',
　　Wid my Bennie 'way from me;
Strangely would my heart be beatin'
　　Tell I knew dat he was free.

When at last he came to table,
　　Neider one could ever bate
Tell in some way we were able
　　To eke out each udder plate:
All me t'oughts were of my frennie
　　Then an' in de after days;
Ne'er can I forget my Bennie
　　Wid him nice an' pleasant ways.

In de evenin' we went walkin',
　　An' de sweet sound of his voice,
As we laughed or kept a-talkin',
　　Made my lovin' heart rejoice:
Full of happiness we strolled on,
　　In de closin' evenin' light,
Where de stately Cobre[1] rolled on
　　Gurglin', murm'rin' in de night;

Where de rushin' cánal waters
　　Splashed t'rough fields of manchinic,

---

[1] the river at Spanish Town.

Wid deir younger tender daughters
  Grow'n' togeder, lush an' t'ick,
Round' de mudder tall an' slimber
  Wid her scalloped leaves o' blue,
In de evenin' light a-limber,
  Or a-tossin' to an' fro.

Back to barracks slowly strollin',[1]
  Leavin' de enticin' soun'
O' de Cobre proudly rollin'
  T'rough de old deserted town ;
Pas' de level well-kept meadows
  O' de spacious prison-land,
Where de twilight's fallin' shadows
  Scattered at de moon's command.

So we passed 'long, half unwillin',
  T'rough de yawnin' barrack-gate,
Our poo' hearts wid disdain fillin'
  O' de life we'd larnt to hate ;
Visions of a turgid ocean
  Of our comrades' noise an' woes,
An' a ne'er-ceasin' commotion
  Sorrowfully 'fo' us rose.

We mixed in de tumult, waitin'
  Fe de moment o' release,
De disorder never 'batin',
  Never 'batin' in de leas' ;
Wid de anger in us growin',
  We grew vexed from black to blue,

---

[1] we slowly strolled.

All de hot blood t'rough us flowin',
   As we hungered for tattoo.

While some o' de men were strong in
   Rum o' Wray an' Nephew fame,
We sat do'n wid ceaseless longin'
   Till at last de tattoo came :
Jes' then we were no more snappy,
   But be'n even in fe fun ;
Once again we felt quite happy
   After de roll-call was done.

Claspin' of our hands togeder,
   Each to each we told good-night,
Dreamed soon o' life's broken ledder
   An' de wul's perplexin' fight,
Of de many souls a-weepin'
   Burdened do'n wid care an' strife,
While we sweetly lay a-sleepin',
   Yet would grumble 'bout our life.

Once his cot was next beside me,
   But dere came misfortune's day
When de pleasure was denied me,
   For de sergeant moved him 'way :
I played not fe mind de movin'
   Though me heart wid grief be'n full ;
'Twas but one kin' o' de provin'
   O' de ways o' dis ya wul'.[1]

---

[1] The reference is to "Whe' fe do?" one of the author's poems in *Songs of Jamaica*.

'Fo' we tu'n good, came de warnin'
  O' de rousin' bugle-soun',
An' you'd see us soon a marnin'
  To de bat'-house hurryin' down,
Leavin' udders yawnin', fumblin',
  Wid deir limbs all stiff an' ole,
Or 'pon stretchin' out an' grumblin',
  Say'n' de water be'n too col'.

In a jiffy we were washin',
  Jeerin' dem, de lazy type,
All about us water dashin'
  Out o' de ole-fashion' pipe:
In a lee while we were endin',—
  Dere was not much time to kill,—
Arms an' bay'nets wanted tendin'
  'Fo' de soon-a-marnin' drill.

So we spent five months togeder,
  He was ever staunch an' true
In sunshine or rainy weader,
  No mind what wrong I would do:
But dere came de sad heart-rendin'
  News dat he must part from me,
An' I nursed my sorrow, bendin'
  To de grim necessity.

All dat week was cold an' dreary,
  An' I worked wid heavy heart;
All my limbs were weak an' weary
  When I knew dat we would part;
All de fond hopes, all de gladness
  Drooped an' faded from our sight,

An' an overwhelmin' sadness
　　Came do'n on de partin' night.

In de dim light I lay thinkin'
　　How dat sad night was our last,
My lone spirit weakly sinkin'
　　'Neat' de mem'ries o' de past :
As I thought in deepest sorrow,
　　He came,—sat do'n by my side,
Speakin' o' de dreaded morrow
　　An' de flow o' life's dark tide.

Gently fell the moonbeams, kissin'
　　'Way de hot tears streamin' free,
While de wind outside went hissin'
　　An' a-moanin' for poor me :
Then he rose, but after bended,
　　Biddin' me a last good-bye ;
To his cot his steps he wended,
　　An' I heard a deep-drawn sigh.

'Twas de same decisive warnin'
　　Wakin' us as in de past,
An' we both washed soon a marnin'
　　'Neat' de ole pipe fe de last ;
We be'n filled wid hollow laughter,
　　Rather tryin' to take heart,
But de grief returned when after
　　Came de moment fe depart.

Hands gripped tight, but not a tear fell
　　As I looked into his face,

Said de final word o' farewell,
  An' returned back to my place:
At my desk I sat me dry-eyed,
  Sometimes gave a low-do'n moan,
An' at moments came a sigh sighed
  For my Bennie dat was gone.

Gone he, de little sunshine o' my life,
Leavin' me 'lone to de Depôt's black strife,
Dear little comrade o' lecture an' drill,
Loved comrade, like me of true stubborn will :
Oft, in de light o' de fast sinkin' sun,
We'd frolic togeder aroun' de big gun ;
Oft would he laughingly run after me,
Chasin' me over de wide Depôt lea ;
Oft would he teach me de folly o' pride
When, me half-vexed, he would sit by my side ;—
Now all is blackness t'rough night an' t'rough day,
For my heart's weary now Bennie's away.

CONSOLATION

I took my marnin' bat' alone,
An' wept for Bennie dat was gone;
An' after,—sittin', weepin' long,—
Some one came askin' wha' be'n wrong:
But only chokin' sobs he heard,
My mout' could never speak a word.
An' so for long days all was grief,
An' never could I get relief;
My heart be'n full of emptiness,
With naught to love an' naught to bless.

I 'member de familiar scene:—
I sat out on de Depôt green,
Restin' agains' de big great gun:
De long rays o' de settin' sun
Were thrown upon the sombre wall;
I heard de rousin' bugle-call
In chorus[1] soundin' o' retreat;
A ray o' light shone on my seat,
A soft dull shade of changin' gold,
So pleasant, lovely to behold:
A moment,—an' I was alone,
De wanin' evenin' sun was gone.

[1] Several bugles together.

23

I sat do'n still ; de evenin' light
Passed on, an' it fell night, dark night.
'Twas autumn : feelin' rather chill,
I rose, led by my aimless will,
An' went up to the second floor,
Sat on a bench agains' de door.
A comrade came an' sat by me,
Restin' a hand upon my knee ;
De lantern old was burnin' dim,
But bright 'nough for me to see him :—
One searchin' look into his face,
I gave him in my heart a place.

I never knew a nicer mind,
He was so pleasant an' so kind ;
An' oh ! the sweetness of his voice
That made my lonely heart rejoice.
It all comes back so vividly,—
The comfort that he brought to me ;
The ray of hope, the pure pure joy
He gave a poor forsaken boy ;
In walk or talk his tender care,
His deep concern for my welfare.
His comin' filled the larger part
Of de great void made in my heart
When on dat cruel awful day
My faithful Bennie went away.

'Tis not de way o' dis ya wul'
Dat any miserable soul
Should know a little lastin' peace,
Should taste endurin' happiness.

De harmless tabby o' de house
Plays kindly wid de frightened mouse,
Till, when it nearly loses dread,
Good Lard! de little thing is dead.
So wid de man, toy of a Will
E'er playin' with him to its fill,
To-day alive, to-morrow slain,—
Thus all our pleasure ends in pain.

Where'er I roam, whate'er the clime,
I'll never know a happier time;
I seemed as happy as could be,
When—everything was torn from me.
De fateful day I 'member still,
De final breakin' o' my will,
Again de sayin' o' good-bye,
My poor heart's silent wailin' cry;
My life, my soul, my all be'n gone,
And ever since I am alone.

FIRE PRACTICE

PAM-PA-PAM, pam-pa-pam, pam-pa-pam,
  Hea' de fire-bugle blow!
Pam-pa-pam, pam-pa-pam, pam-pa-pam,
  Depôt boys, tu'n do'n below!

Runnin' do'n out o' de big barrack-room,
  Haulin' de two engine out o' de shed;
Formin' up into a long double line,
  Wait tell de fus' wud o' cómmand is said.

Soon as we hea' it we start t'rough de gate,
  Wid buckets, ledder, an' engine an' key:
Joyously happy, with right cheery will
  Tramp we away from de big Depôt lea.

Whole line in twos we go marchin' along,
  List'nin' de tramp-trampin' tune of our feet,
Side winks a-givin' our gals as we pass
  Merrily, nimbly along White Church Street.

At de shrill soun' o' de whistle we halt,
  An' when de engine an' all is fixed square,
We start a-pumpin' wid might an' wid main,
  Sendin' clear water chock up in de air.

Pumpin' an' pumpin' an' pumpin' away,
  Pumpin' in earnest, yet pumpin' wid fun,
Once more again by de whistle we stop,—
  An' den de day's fire-practice is done.

Pam-pa-pam, pam-pa-pam, pam-pa-pam,
  Hea' de fire-bugle blow!
Pam-pa-pam, pam-pa-pam, pam-pa-pam,
  Depôt boys, tu'n do'n below!

NOTE.—The first and last stanzas go to the following tune in F, two-four time: 1st bar; crotchet rest, quaver rest, 2 semiquavers C third space. 2nd bar; quaver C, 2 semiquavers A (the 3rd below), 2 semiquavers F (3rd below again). 3rd bar; crotchet F, quaver rest, 2 semiquavers C (middle C). 4th bar; 2 semiquavers F, 2 semiquavers middle C, crotchet F. 5th bar; same as 1st; 6th, same as 2nd; 7th, same as 3rd. 8th bar; dotted quaver F, semi-quaver F, dotted quaver middle C, semiquaver middle C. 9th bar; minim F.

SECOND-CLASS CONSTABLE ALSTON

I WATCHED him as his cheek grew pale,
He that once was strong and hale;
The red had faded all away,
And left it ashen, dull and gray.

One Monday night he came to me,
Rested his head upon my knee:
"O Mac, me feel so sick," he said,
"I t'ink me poor boy soon wi' dead."

I did my best to calm his fears,
He opened up his breast in tears;
I'll ne'er forget the sight I saw,
His body strewn with bumps—all raw.

That night we listened to his moans,
The hot fever was in his bones;
He tossed and tossed about until,
All his strength spent, he lay down still.

Many a weary weary day
In the hospital he lay,
Till one morn torture turned to peace,
For death had brought him his release.

The funeral, oh it was grand !
We honoured him with arms and band ;
And not a man but turned away
Wet-eyed from where his comrade lay.

LAST WORDS OF THE DYING RECRUIT

Where's you' tender han', mumma,
Dat would fingle up me jaw
When de fever burned so deep,
An' A couldn' get no sleep?

Where's de voice me love' to hear
Whisp'rin' sweetest words o' cheer?—
Voice dat taught me A B C
As me leaned 'pon mumma's knee.

Look de 'panish-needle grass
Growin' by de gully pass !
Is dat fe me ducky hen
Cacklin' roun'-a rabbit pen?

Hea' de John-t'whits in-a glee
Singin' in de mammee tree !
Listen, comin' up de dale
Chirpin's o' de nightingale !

All de chune dem die away :—
Do you see de shinin' ray
On da' tiny buttercup?
'Tis de sun a-comin' up.

30

Now's full time fe me to wake,
'Causen we ha' bread fe bake;
Git up, Sam, you lazy wretch,
For de beas' dem fe go ketch:

Ef you 'low de sun fe grow,[1]
Grass-lice wi' sure mek you know;
S'arch up to de ole-groun' side,
For de jack wi' 'tan' deh hide.

Mumma, me wan' go a school,
Te-day we gwin' play tom-fool:
Quick!   Gi'e me my book an' slate,
For I doana want fe late.

Sister, wha' de doctor t'ink?
Say mumma a lower sink?
Lard! ef she gwin' go lef' we,
Wha' de use o' life fe me?

Sister, sister, a no true,
Mumma caan' dis dead 'way so;
Sister, sister, leave me 'lone,
Me won' bélieve dat she gone.

Ah! no fe her own han' now
Restin' on me fevered brow?
Mumma, lay me 'pon you' breas',
Mek me get a drop o' res'.

[1] See glossary, under "Ef."

Mumma!—a whe' mumma deh?
Mumma!—mumma gone away?
Gone, oh gone is eberyt'ing,
But de funny fancies cling.

Aye, t'enk God, me mumma come!
Ma, no lef' me, tek me home;
Tek me from de awful strife
Of dis miserable life.

BOUND FE DUTY

TRAMP, tramp, tramp, we go a-trampin',
    Pólicemen on duty boun'
From de Depôt to de city,
    For dere's racin'-time come roun'.

Wid our great cloaks buttoned round we,
    Our best trampin' boots all strong,
Kit-bags, helmet-bags in each hand,
    We go merrily along.

Tramp, tramp, tramp, we go a-trampin',
    Stoutly marchin' t'rough de rain;
Soon we'll all be tucked quite snugly
    In a corner o' de train.

Our light hearts are filled wid gladness,
    As we're sweetly whirled awáy
From de station to de city,
    For it means some extra pay.

Passin' cane-fields all a-racin',
    Lush bananas coated blue,
We're whirled onward to de city,
    Where dere's work for us to do.

BUMMING

Of all de people I don't like,
  A chief one is de bummer;
He bums around from morn to night
  T'rough winter an' t'rough summer.

Ef we should go aroun' John's shop,
  An' he ketch scent o' rum's up,
You'll soon see'm pokin' up him nose
  Wid him bare-face an' comes-up.

Ef we are smokin' cigarette,
  He wants a part of it too;
An' ebery bluff you gi'e to him,
  He's answer got to fit you.

Anedder thing I really hate
  Is, when de touris' come in,
To see some people flockin' dem,
  An' ebery one a-bummin'.

I think it is an ugly sight
  To see a bummin' bobby;
Yet plenty o' dem tek it for
  A precious piece of hobby.[1]

[1] Many of them make it their favourite practice.

I proud 'nuff o' me uniform
   Not ever to be rummy ;
Much mo' fe lower do'n mese'f
   An' mek my min' feel bummy.

If people like to see somet'ing,
   It is a bobby quaffin'
A glass or two o' common rum,—
   Then drunk,—dey start a-laughin'.

I tell you, all my comrades dear,
   Dough your pay might be little,
Don't cringe an' fawn 'fore richer men,
   Deir pelf's not wort' a tittle.

My pay is small, an' yet I live
   An' feel proud as a lord too ;
Ef you'll be men you soon will find
   How much it can reward you.

De honest toil is pure as gold,
   An' he who wuks a penny
Can mek his life as much wort' while
   As he who earns a guinea.

Our trouble is dat those above
   Do oftentimes oppress ;
But we'll laugh at or pity dem,
   Or hate dem mo' or less.

So we mus' mek de best o' t'ings,
 An' never be too rummish ;
'Twill help us many ways, an' 'top
 Us all from bein' bummish.

DE DOG-DRIVER'S FRIEN'

STAY your hasty hands, my comrades,
   I must speak to you again;
For you beat de dog 'dout mussy,
   An' dey are we night-time frien'.
Treat dem kindly, treat dem kindly,
   For dey are God's creatures too;
You have no more claim, dear comrades,
   On de earth dan what dey do.

'Cos you locked him up in barracks
   T'rough some failin' point o' his,
You mus' beatin' him so badly
   For de little carelessness?
Treat dem kindly, etc.

When de hours are cold an' dreary,
   An' I'm posted on me beat,
An' me tired heavy body
   Weighs upon me weary feet;

When I think of our oppressors
   Wid mixed hatred an' don'-care,
An' de ugly miau of tom-puss
   Rings out sharply on de air,

Oftentimes dem come aroun' me
　Wid dem free an' trusting soul,
Lying do'n or gambolling near me
　Wid a tender sort o' gro'l :

An' I snap my fingers at them,
　While dey wag dem tail at me ;
Can you wonder dat I love dem,
　Dem, me night-time company ?
Treat dem kindly, etc.

Sometimes dey're a bit too noisy
　Wid deir long leave-taking bark ;[1]
But I tell you what, it cheers me
　When de nights are extra dark.

So, dear comrades, don't ill-treat him,
　You won't mek me talk in vain ;
'Member, when de hours are dreary,
　He's de poor dog-driver's frien'.
Treat dem kindly, etc.

---

[1] This is a trick of the dogs when they want to leave their master's yard. They set up a great barking about 11 p.m., as if they were on the alert, and soon after they are all gone.

TO INSPECTOR W. E. CLARK

(ON HIS RETURN)

We welcome you, dear Sir, again ;
But oh ! de comin' brings us pain,
For though we greet you glad to-day,
Once more you're bound to go away :
We grieve now deeper than before
To know you'll be wid us no more.

We t'ought o' meetin' you in gladness ;
But no, our hearts are filled with sadness
To learn *why* we must part from you,
An officer so dear an' true :
Our prayer is dat de Fates will bless
You an' your kin wid health an' peace.

Farewell, dear Sir, farewell again !—
A farewell fraught wi' deepest pain :
De very ringin' o' de bell
Sounds like a wailin' of farewell ;
We feel it deeply, to de core,
To know you'll be wid us no more.

PAPINE CORNER

When you want to meet a frien',
  Ride up to Papine,
Where dere's people to no en',
  Old, young, fat an' lean:
When you want nice gals fe court
  An' to feel jus' booze',
Go'p to Papine as a sport
  Dress' in ge'man clo'es.

When you want to be jus' broke,
  Ride up wid your chum,
Buy de best cigars to smoke
  An' Finzi old rum:
Stagger roun' de sort o' square
  On to Fong Kin bar;
Keep as much strengt' dat can bear
  You do'n in de car.

When you want know Sunday bright,
  Tek a run up deh
When 'bout eight o'clock at night
  Things are extra gay:
Ef you want to see it cram',
  Wait tell night is dark,
An' beneat' your breat' you'll damn
  Coney Island Park.

40

When you want see gals look fine,
    You mus' go up dere,
An' you'll see them drinkin' wine
    An' all sorts o' beer :
There you'll see them walkin' out,
    Each wid a young man,
Watch them strollin' all about,
    Flirtin' all dem can.

When you want hear coarsest jokes
    Passin' rude an' vile,
Want to see de Kingston blokes,—
    Go up dere awhile :
When you want hear murderin'
    On de piano,
An' all sorts o' drunken din,
    Papine you mus' go.

Ef you want lost póliceman,
    Go dere Sunday night,
Where you'll see them, every one
    Lookin' smart an' bright :
Policeman of every rank,
    Rural ones an' all,
In de bar or on de bank,
    Each one in them sall.

Policeman dat's in his beat,
    Policeman widout,
Policeman wid him gold teet'
    Shinin' in him mout' ;

Policeman in uniform
  Made of English blue,
P'liceman gettin' rather warm,
  Sleuth policeman too.

Policeman on plain clo'es pass,
  Also dismissed ones;
See them standin' in a mass,
  Talkin' 'bout them plans:
Policeman " struck off de strengt'
  Physical unfit,"
Hear them chattin' dere at lengt'
  'Bout a diffran' kit.

When you want meet a surprise,
  Tek de Papine track;
Dere some things will meet you' eyes
  Mek you tu'n you' back:
When you want to see mankind
  Of " class " family
In a way degra' them mind,
  Go 'p deh, you will see.

When you want a pleasant drive,
  Tek Hope Gardens line;
I can tell you, man alive,
  It is jolly fine:
Ef you want to feel de fun,
  You mus' only wait
Until when you're comin' do'n
  An' de tram is late.

DISILLUSIONED[1]

Can you leave me so, my Dan,
Can you leave you' little Fan
'Ter all o' me lub fe you?—
An' my heart is still true, true.

Can you leave me, leave me so,
Full me heart wid grief an' woe,
Leave me to a bitter fate,
When I'm in dis awful state?

'Member you de days gone by
When for me you said you'd die?
How you let me see you' heart,
Vowing we could never part?

'Member you my foolish pride
When we be'n up mountain-side?
How you go do'n 'pon you' knee,
Sayin' you'd be true to me?

An' I followed you away
Do'n to dis ya dreary bay;
Fool to lef' me mudder's home,
When she said me shouldn' come!

[1] Sequel to " My Pretty Dan " in *Songs of Jamaica*.

Now, sake ob a to'n-bred miss,
You mus' treat me laka dis!
Tramplin' me under you' feet,
Tu'nin' me out in de street.

Will she warm you when you're chill?
Will you get of lub you' fill?
Will she starve herse'f fe you,
As I always use' fe do?

Will a to'n gal go bare-feet,
Jes' fe try mek two ends meet?
Will she car' water an' wash,
Jes' fe help out you' lee cash?

Is she sweet an' undefile'
As you took me, jes' a chil',
'Fo' I knew about de wul',
Gave to you my pure pure soul?

Will you leave me all forlorn
'Fo' de lilly baby's born?—
Who wi' eber tek me in
Wid dis dreadful load o' sin?

Foolish, foolish young gals who
T'ink a constab could be true!
Foolish, foolish every one
Who will trus' a póliceman!

Dem wi' ondly try fe rob
All de good you mighta hab ;
An' 'fo' you can count de cost,
You wi' find you'se'f lost, lost.

Will you leave me, heartless Dan,
For a risky to'n woman ?
When I'm burdened do'n wid woe,
Will you leave me, leave me so ?

COTCH DONKEY

Ko how de jackass
   Lay do'n in de road ;
An' him ondly car'
   Little bit o' load.

Kue, jackass, git up !
   'Tan' up 'pon you' foot !
Dis ya load no load,
   You's a lazy brut'.

Me no know wha' mek
   Pa won' swop you too ;
For dere's not a t'ing
   Wut while you can do.

Ef you car' no load,
   It is all de same ;
Hamper on or no,
   'Tis de ushal game.

Póliceman a come
   Fe go mek a row,
All because o' you
   Wid you' wutless now.

" See ya, Sah, no min',
　Dis a fe me luck ;
De jackass is bad,
　Him no wan' fe wuk.

" ' Tek de hamper off ? '
　Him no hab no cut :
Me deh tell you say
　De jackass no wut.

" Lard ! me Gahd o' me !
　Him got one lee 'cratch :
Dat is not'in', Sah,
　For him always cotch.

Do, Sah, let me off,
　Ef fe te-day one[1] ;
For a no de 'cratch
　Cause him fe lay do'n."

Now because o' you
　Dem gone bring me up ;[2]
An' wha' hu't me mos',
　You caan' wuk a tup.

Ef dem summons me,
　Mek me pay few mac,
Dat caan' mek me 'top
　Wuk you wid sore back.

[1] Just this once.　　[2] They have gone to get out a summons.

ME WHOPPIN' BIG-TREE BOY

I'M aweary weary standin', wid me heart chock-full o'
grief,
An' a great lump in me bosom, an' A canna' get
relief:
Walkin' up an' do'n de road, I see a whoppin' Syrian-
boy,
An' I grudge him, yes I grudge him for his heart so
full o' joy.

'Twas a hot, hot day o' brain-work, an' me heart was
sick an' sad,
As I staggered 'long de car-line, but de boy's cheek
made me glad:
Wid his han's dem set akimbo in a mannish sort o'
way,
Said he "Do wha' it you like, but A wi' wuk no mo'
te-day."

An' de Syrian grew astonished as he looked upon his
load,
Which de whoppin' big-tree boy had tumbled in de
middle road:
He was boun' fe Lawrence Tavern, business called
him dere to-night,
An' he begged his ole-time carrier jes' to help him
out his plight.

"Nummo wuk at all fe me is my determination still;
Me no care damn wha' you say, an' you can jes' do
    wha' you will:
Me deh go right back to to'n, yah, underneat' me old
    big-tree;
All dem boys wid eboe-light dem, dem is waitin' deh
    fe me.

"Now I'm free fe talk abouten all de people whe' you
    rob,
How you sell wha' no wut gill self to black naygur for
    a bob;
But me eboe-light wi' sure talk, of dat you can have
    no doubt,
Fe revenge de quantity o' poor poor people you play out.

"Jes' becausen say dem poo' so, an' t'rough poverty
    dem mus'
Tek a couple o' t'ings from you dat you're trick
    enough fe trus',
You robbin' dem so badly;[1] but A sorry fe you
    dough,
How we boys beneat' de big-tree really mean fe mek
    you know."

Then I roared, I roared with laughter, although
    posted on my beat,
Till I half forgot de sore pain in me bosom an' my feet:
Ah! I wish I knew a little, jes' a little of de joy
Dat Nature has bestowed on you, my whoppin' big-
    tree boy.

[1] This should be read almost as if it were a question.

D

A RECRUIT ON THE CORPY

Me an' de corpy drink we rum,
An' corpy larn me how fe bum;
Last night me gie 'm de last-last tup,
Yet now him come an' bring me up.

He'll carry me 'fo' officer,
An' rake up' t'ings fe charge me for;
An' all because dese couple days
Me couldn' gie 'm dɜ usual raise.

Last night, when it come to roll-call,
Dis corpy couldn' 'ten' at all:
We didn' mek de S.M. see 'm,
But only put things 'traight fe him.

An' we, like big fools, be'n deh fret
Ober de corpy drunk to deat':
We all treat him so very kin',
Aldough him ha' such dutty min'.

We tek him drunken off de car,
We tek him drunken out de bar,
We wake him drunken 'pon him guard,
An' yet we neber claim reward.

All bad contráry things me do,
Corpy see me an' let me go ;
But 'causen me no ha' a tup,
Fe not'in' 'tall him bring me up.

PAY-DAY

Dere's a little anxious crowd
  Jes' outside de barrack gate,
All a-t'inkin' deir own way
  Dat de pay is kept back late:
Faces of all types an' shades,
  Brown an' yaller, black an' gray,
Dey are waitin', waitin' dere,
  For it's póliceman pay-day.

Clearly seen among dem all
  Is a colourless white face
Anxious more dan every one,
  Fine type of an alien race:
He is waitin' for some cash
  On de goods trust' tarra day,—
Our good frien' de Syrian,—
  For it's policeman pay-day.

Wid a lee piece of old clot'
  'Pon her curly glossy hair,
Print frock an' old bulldog boots
  Tatters all t'rough wear an' tear,
She is waitin', ober-bex',
  Our mess-woman, mudder Mell,
An' 'twould grieve you' heart to hear
  'Bouten wha' she's got to tell.

Six long fortnight come an' gone
   Since some constab hol' her up,
An', wid all de try she try,
   She can neber get a tup :
" Me wi' tell Inspector F——
   'Bout de 'ole o' i' to-day,
An' den me wi' really see
   Ef him caan' boun' dem fe pay.

" Man dem, wid dem hungry gut,
   Six long fortnight nyam me rash ;
Not a gill me caan' get when
   Chiny dah dun fe him cash
Fe de plenty t'ings me trus',
   Sal' fish, pork, an' flour, an' rice,
Onion an' ingredients,
   Jes' fe mek de brukfus' nice."

See de waitin' midnight girl
   Wid her saucy cock-up lips,
An' her strongly-built black hands
   Pressed against her rounded hips :
She has passed de bound'ry line,
   An' her womanhood is sold ;
Wonder not then, as you gaze,
   Dat, though young, she looks so bold.

Once she roamed de country woods
   Wid a free an' stainless soul,
But she left for Kingston's slums,
   Gave herself up to de wul':

She has trod de downward course,
　Never haltin' on de way;
Dere's no better time for her
　Dan a póliceman pay-day.

Waits de slimber ball-pan man,
　Waits de little ice-cream lad,
Waits our washerwoman Sue,—
　All deh chat how pólice bad;
Each one sayin' police vile,
　Yet deir faces all betray
Dat for dem dere's no rag time
　Laka policeman pay-day.

Inside in de ord'ly room
　Things are movin' very fine;
Constab standin' in a row
　Hea' de jinglin' o' de coin;
Constab wid a solemn face,
　Constab only full o' fun,
Marchin' in de ord'ly room
　As dem name call one by one.

Quick march!—halt!—a sharp right tu'n,
　Wid de right han' smart salute,
All attention poker-stiff,
　An' a-standin' grave an' mute:
Office-clerk calls out de name,
　Officer hands de amount
To Sa'an' Major standin' by,
　Who gives it a second count.

'Ter all de formalities,
  Dis an' dat an' warra not,
Salute,—'tion,—right about turn,—
  Den de precious pay is got :
Lee gone to de réward fund
  T'rough a blot' defaulter-sheet,
Run do'n by sub-officers,
  Or caught sleepin' on dem beat ;

Den dere's somet'ing gone fe kit ;
  Uniform mus' smart an' nice,
Else de officer won' t'ink
  Dat a bobby's wutten price.
All dem way de money go ;
  So de payin'-out fe some,
When de fortnight dem come roun',
  Bégin in-a ord'ly room.

Now comes payin' up de debts
  To de miscellaneous crowd
Waitin' by de barrack-gate,
  Chattin', chattin' very loud :
Payin', payin' all de time,
  From a poun' do'n to a gill,
Whole fortnight-pay partly done,
  Yet rum-money lef' back still.

Strollin' t'rough de gate at night,
  Drinkin' Finzi tell dead drunk,
Barely standin' at tattoo,—
  After[1] tumblin' in-a bunk ;

[1] Afterwards.

All de two-an'-four is done,
So-so trust nong ebery day
Tell de fortnight comes again
An' we get de little pay.

THE APPLE-WOMAN'S COMPLAINT

WHILE me deh walk 'long in de street,
Policeman's yawnin' on his beat;
An' dis de wud him chiefta'n say—
Me mus'n' car' me apple-tray.

Ef me no wuk, me boun' fe tief;
S'pose dat will please de pólice chief!
De prison dem mus' be wan' full,[1]
Mek dem's 'pon we like ravin' bull.

Black nigger wukin' laka cow
An' wipin' sweat-drops from him brow,
Dough him is dyin' sake o' need,
P'lice an' dem headman boun' fe feed.

P'lice an' dem headman gamble too,
Dey shuffle card an' bet fe true;
Yet ef me Charlie gamble,—well,
Dem try fe 'queeze him laka hell.

De headman fe de town police
Mind[2] neber know a little peace,

---

[1] The prisons must want occupants, and that is why they are
down upon us like angry bulls.
[2] The mind of the chief of the town police is never happy,
except, etc.

'Cep' when him an' him heartless ban'
Hab sufferin' nigger in dem han'.

Ah son-son! dough you 're bastard, yah,
An' dere's no one you can call pa,
Jes' try to ha' you' mudder's min'
An' Police Force you'll neber jine.

But how judge bélieve pólicemen,
Dem dutty mout' wid lyin' stain'?
While we go batterin' along
Dem doin' we all sort o' wrong.

We hab fe barter-out we soul
To lib t'rough dis ungodly wul';—
O massa Jesus! don't you see
How pólice is oppressin' we?

Dem wan' fe see we in de street
Dah foller dem all 'pon dem beat;
An' after, 'dout a drop o' shame,
Say we be'n dah solicit dem.

Ah massa Jesus! in you' love
Jes' look do'n from you' t'rone above,
An' show me how a poo' weak gal
Can lib good life in dis ya wul'.

KNUTSFORD PARK RACES

Batch o' p'licemen, lookin' fine,
Tramp away to de car line;
No more pólicemen can be
Smart as those from Half Way Tree:
Happy, all have happy faces,
For 'tis Knutsford Park big races.

No room in de tram fe stan':
"Oh! de races will be gran',—
Wonder ef good luck we'll hab,
Get fe win a couple bob!"
Joyous, only joyous faces,
Goin' to de Knutsford races.

Motor buggy passin' by,
Sendin' dus' up to de sky;
P'licemen, posted diffran' place,
Buy dem ticket on de race:
Look now for de anxious faces
At de Knutsford Park big races!

Big-tree boys a t'row dem dice:
"P'lice te-day no ha' no v'ice,—

All like we,[1] so dem caan' mell,—
Mek we gamble laka hell ":
Rowdy, rowdy-looking faces
At de Knutsford Park big races.

Ladies white an' brown an' black,
Fine as fine in gala frock,
Wid dem race-card in dem han'
Pass 'long to de dollar stan':
Happy-lookin' lady faces
At de Knutsford Park big races.

Ge'men wid dem smart spy-glass,
Well equip' fe spot dem harse,
Dress' in Yankee-fashion clo'es,
Watch de flag as do'n it goes :
Oh ! de eager, eager faces
At de Knutsford Park big races !

Faces of all types an' kinds,
Faces showin' diffran' minds,
Faces from de udder seas—
Right from de antipodes :
Oh ! de many various faces
Seen at Knutsford Park big races !

Jockeys lookin' quite dem bes',
In deir racin' clo'es all dress'

---

[1] All are doing as we do.

(Judge de feelin's how dem proud)
Show de harses to de crowd :
Now you'll see de knowin' faces
At de Knutsford Park big races.

Soldier ban', formed in a ring,
Strike up " God save our king ";
Gub'nor come now by God's grace
To de Knutsford Park big race :
High faces among low faces
At de Knutsford Park big races.

Ladies, 'teppin' up quite cool,
Buy dem tickets at de pool ;
Dough 'tis said he's got a jerk,
Dere's no harse like Billie Burke :
Look roun' at de cock-sure faces
At de Knutsford Park big races.

Hey ! de flag is gone do'n, oh !
Off at grips de harses go !
Dainty's leadin' at a boun',
Stirrup-cup is gainin' ground' :
Strainin', eager strainin' faces
At de Knutsford Park big races.

Last day o' de race—all's done,
An' de course is left alone ;
Everybody's goin' home,
Some more light dan when dey'd come :
Oh ! de sad, de bitter faces
After Knutsford Park big races !

THE HEART OF A CONSTAB

'TIS hatred without an' 'tis hatred within,
    An' I am so weary an' sad;
For all t'rough de tempest o' terrible strife
    Dere's not'in' to make poor me glad.

Oh! where are de faces I loved in de past,
    De frien's dat I used to hold dear?
Oh say, have dey all turned away from me now
    Becausen de red seam I wear?

I foolishly wandered away from dem all
    To dis life of anguish an' woe,
Where I mus' be hard on me own kith an' kin,
    And even to frien' mus' prove foe.

Oh! what have I gained from my too too rash act
    O' joinin' a hard Constab Force,
Save quenchin' me thirst from a vinegar cup,
    De vinegar cup o' remorse?

I t'ought of a livin' o' pure honest toil,
    To keep up dis slow-ebbin' breath;
But no, de life surely is bendin' me do'n,
    Is bendin' me do'n to de death.

'Tis grievous to think dat, while toilin' on here,
  My people won't love me again,
My people, my people, me owna black skin,—
  De wretched t'ought gives me such pain.

But I'll leave it, my people, an' come back to you,
  I'll flee from de grief an' turmoil ;
I'll leave it, though flow'rs here should line my
        path yet,
  An' come back to you an' de soil.

For 'tis hatred without an' 'tis hatred within,
  An' how can I live 'douten heart ?
Then oh for de country, de love o' me soul,
  From which I shall nevermore part !

FE ME SAL

In de blazin' midday heat, when I'm posted on me beat,
  Who I t'inkin' of but fe me Sal?
She is eber in me mind, ne'er a better you will find,
  She's me only lub, de best o' country gal.

When I started out fe roam from me treasured moun-
    tain-home,
  All me wanderin's were for her good;
A be'n ondly fe her sake why dis job I undertake,
  An' she cheer me when I'm sad an' out o' mood.

Any wuk I'm put to do, me jes' feel she's wid me too,
  Biddin' me fe toil bedouten fret;
An' when all de duty's done, an' me go to sleep alone,
  'Tis but dreamin' o' me darlin' little pet.

When me deh 'pon station guard, dere is ondly one
    reward,
  For I get fe write her sweet lub-wuds;
Den me finish up her name wid a pile o' flourish dem,
  An' me seal de letter up wid jesmy buds.

When me go patrol a day, she's me one lee bit o' stay
  As A deh climb up Bardowie hill;
An' A somehow favour know dat, wherever I may go,
  Her soul an' heart wi' eber be mine still.
64

Ef me goin' to de race I'm a-t'inkin' of her face,
  An' A feel her shedah at me side;
Ef me eatin' me lee grub, I'm a-t'inkin' o' de lub
  Dat me ha' fe her alone so free an' wide.

Udder p'liceman ha' dem gal, but dere's none like fe
     me Sal,
  Dey can neber trus' fe dem like me;
And I needn't eber fear, ef I'm transferred anywhere,
  For me Sally is as true as true can be.

She's de darlin' o' me life, an' shall one day be me
     wife
  Jes' as soon as eberyt'ing is ripe;
An' me hab a feelin' strong dat it will not be too long
  'Fo' me get fe wear an Acting Corp'ral's stripe.

She's de darlin' o' me heart, an' we'll neber neber part,
  She's de prettiest black gal in de wul';
An' whereber you may go you won't find anedder so,
  Wid more tender min' an' better sort o' soul.

So de day shall soon arrive when de two o' we shall
     drive
  To de parish church at Half Way Tree:
An' we'll stroll back t'rough de gate, me Sal a corpy's
     mate,
  An' we'll be as happy-happy as can be.

E

THE BOBBY TO THE SNEERING LADY

You may sneer at us, madam,
    But our work is beastly hard;
An' while toilin thus we scarce
    Ever get a lee reward.

Our soul's jes' like fe you,
    If our work does make us rough;
Me won't 'res' you servant-gal
    When you've beaten her enough.

You may say she is me frien',
    We are used to all such prate;
Naught we meet on life's stern road
    But de usual scorn an' hate.

Say dat you wi' 'port me, ma'am?
    I was lookin' fe dat,—well,
Our Inspector's flinty hard,
    'Twill be few days' pay or cell.

Pains an' losses of such kind
    To we p'licemen's not'in' new;
Still A'd really like fe hear
    Wha' good it wi' do to you.

66

Last week, eatin' a gill bread,
   Me t'row piece out on de lea;
An' A ketch a 'port fe dat
   Which meant five roun' mac to me.

Constab-charge, civilian-charge,
   Life's a burden every way;
But reward fund[1] mus' kep' up
   Out o' poo' policeman pay.

Ef our lot, then, is so hard,
   I mus' ever bear in mind
Dat to fe me own black 'kin
   I mus' not be too unkind.

An' p'r'aps you too will forgive
   Ef I've spoken rather free,
An' will let me somet'ing ask
   Which may soften you to me:

In de middle o' de night,
   When de blackness lies do'n deep,
Who protects your homes an' stores
   While de Island is asleep?

When de dead stars cannot shine
   Sake o' rain an' cloud an' storm,
Who keeps watch out in de street
   So dat not'in' comes to harm?

[1] A fund out of which rewards are given to constables for
meritorious work.

Ah ! you turn away your head !
See ! dere's pity in your face !
Don't, dear madam, bring on me
This unmerited disgrace.

THE MALINGERER

Me mus' wukin overdue,
   An' 'tis all because o' you ;
Me mus' wuk hard laka dis
   'Counten o' you' wutlessness.

'Tis a dutty sort o' trick,
   Ebery duty-time you sick ;
An' 'tis always my bad luck
   Fe detail fe extra wuk.

Night off ágain me won' get,
   Dese t'ings mek a poo' man fret,
An' feel him could not do worse
   Dan fe go join Police Force.

Hospital a fe you bed ;
   God knows wha mek you won' dead !
Doctor no know how fe do,
   Else dem wouldan p'ison you.

An' me know man dyin' out,
   Yet de doctor dem would doubt,
Dough he's weak in ebery limb,
   Dat a t'ing was wrong wid him.

Yet you dih-ya 'douten use,
  Only formin' like de juice ;
An' dem caan' see, se'p me king,
  Dat you 'pon malingering.

Ef a money you dah sabe,
  Better min' de open grabe[1] :
T'enk God ! new rule come te-day,
  Hospital bud gets no pay.

Me wi' really beat de eight,
  But you mark me wud—an' wait !
Your time's comin' soon—don't doubt—
  When you'll also be kicked out.

[1] Although you are saving messing expenses, etc., yet you may catch "hospital sick" (sickness) and die of it ; and then of what use is your money ?

A LABOURER'S LIFE GIVE ME

I was never ashamed o' de soil,
   So you needn't remind me of it;
I was born midst de moil an' de toil,
   An' I'll never despise it a bit.

"Sen' me back to de cutliss an' hoe!"
   I don't mind, Sir, a wud dat you say,
For little, it seems, you do know
   Of de thing dat you sneer at to-day.

If I'd followed a peasant's career,
   I would now be a happier lad;
You would not be abusing me here,
   An' mekin' me sorry an' sad.

Fool! I hated my precious birthright,
   Scornin' what made my father a man;
Now I grope in de pitchy dark night,
   Hate de day when me poo' life began.

To de loved country life I'll return,
   I don't mind at all, Sir, if you smile;
As a peasant my livin' I'll earn,
   An' a labourer's life is worth while.

As a labourer livin' content,
　　Wid at night a rest-place for me head,
Oh ! how gaily my life will be spent,
　　Wid de baneful ambition gone dead.

An' when, after a day's wukin' hard,
　　I go home to a fait'ful wifee,
For my toilin' dere'll be its reward,
　　A peaceful heart happy an' free.

An' me children shall grow strong an' true,
　　But I'll teach dem dat life is a farce,
An' de best in dis wul' dey can do
　　Is to bear with content its sad cross.

So I'll make meself happy at home,
　　An' my life will be pleasanter yet ;
I will take de hard knocks as dey come,
　　But will conquer de worry an' fret.

Oh ! a labourer's life's my desire
　　In de hot sun an' pure season rains,
When de glow o' de dark-red bush fire
　　Sends a new blood a-flow'n' t'rough me veins.

FREE

Scarce can I believe my eyes,
Yet before me there it lies,
Precious paper granting me
Quick release from misery.

So farewell to Half Way Tree,
And the plains I hate to see!
Soon will I forget my ills
In my loved Clarendon hills.

COMRADES FOUR

DEAR comrades, my comrades,
　My heart is always true;
An' ever an' ever
　I shall remember you.

We all joined together,
　Together joined we four;
An' I have been first to
　Pass t'rough the open door.[1]

We four drilled together,
　Together drilled we all;
An' I've been the first to
　Flee from the life o' gall.

We parted, dear comrades,
　We parted all in tears,
An' each went his own way
　To shoulder life's sad cares.

O comrades, my comrades,
　What is de lasting gain,
But all t'rough de tempest
　A heart of unmixed pain?

---

[1] In allusion to the writer's discharge.

My comrades, loved comrades,
  I hear your bitter cry;
But life's pain will end, boys,
  Will end yet—by an' by.

TO W. G. G.

Come, come wid me, my tired soul,
'Way from de miserable wul';
Come from de noise, de wild alarm,
To heights o' mountain peace an' calm.

Do you not hear de battle's roar,
De tumult ragin' on de shore?
Do you not see de poisonous bait
Man sets for man t'rough deadly hate?

Come flee de envy an' de strife,
Before dey ruin our life:
Come to de hills; dey may be drear,
But we can shun de evil here.

De northers now are blowin' chill,
De fog hangs dismal on de hill,
An' sometimes fe long dreary days
De sun is wrapt up in-a haze.

De season rain is on te-day,
De flowers all are fadin' 'way;
But dere 'll be sun upon de heights
After de gloomy Christmas nights.

76

Soon shall we feel de heartening charm
Of country life, de sunshine warm ;
An' see, wherever we may roam,
Wild flowers burstin' into bloom.

We'll hear de murmur o' de rills,
We'll clearly see de verdant hills
Wid here an' dere de peasant's field
So lovely in its fruitful yield.

De helpless playt'ing of a Will,
We'll spend our short days here ; an' still,
Though prisoners, feel somehow free
To live our lives o' misery.

Dear comrade o' de constab life,
I've gone an' left you in de strife ;
But whether skies are dark or blue,
Dis true true heart remembers you.

SUKEE RIVER[1]

I SHALL love you ever,
    Dearest Sukee River:
Dash against my broken heart,
Nevermore from you I'll part,
    But will stay forever,
    Crystal Sukee River.

    Cool my fevered brow:
    Ah! 'tis better now,
As I serpent-like lance t'rough
Your broad pool o' deepest blue!
    Dis once burnin' brow
    Is more better now.

    All about me dashin',
    H'is'in' up an' splashin',
Bubbles like de turtle-berries,
Jostlin' wid de yerry-yerries,
    All about me dashin'
    H'is'in' up an' splashin'.

    Oh! dis blissful swim,
    Like a fairy dream!

---

[1] A river in Clarendon. Pronounce *Sooky*, with *oo* as in *look*.

Jumpin' off de time-worn plank,
Pupperlicks from bank to bank,
  Dis delightful swim
  Is a fairy dream.

  Kiss my naked breast
  In its black skin drest:
Let your dainty silver bubbles
Ease it of its lifelong troubles,
  Dis my naked breast
  In its black skin drest.

  Floatin', floatin' down
  On my back alone,
Kiss me on my upturned face,
Clasp me in your fond embrace,
  As I'm floatin' down
  Happy, yet alone.

  Wavelets laughin' hound me,
  Ripples glad surround me:
Catchin' at dem light an' gay,
See dem scamper all away,
  As dey playful hound me,
  Or in love surround me.

  T'rough de twistin' dance
  Onward do I lance:
Onward under yonder cave
Comes wid me a pantin' wave,
  Speedin' from de dance
  Wid me as I lance.

'Neat' dis shadin' hedge
  Growin' by your bridge,
I am thinkin' o' you' love,
Love dat not'in' can remove,
  'Neat' dis shadin' hedge
  Growin' by your bridge.

  Love more pure, I ken,
    Dan de love o' men,
Knowin' not de fickle mind
Nor de hatred o' my kind ;
    Purer far, I ken,
    Dan de love o' men.

  E'en when welcome deat'
    Claims dis painful breat',
Of you I will ever think
Who first gave me crystal drink ;
    E'en when welcome deat'
    Claims dis painful breat'.

  For a little while
    I must leave your smile :
Raindrops fallin' from de sky
Force me now to say good-bye ;
    Jes' lee bit o' while
    I must leave your smile.

  Foamin' Sukee River,
    Dearer now dan ever,
I'll ne'er roam from you again
To a life o' so-so pain,
    Crystal flowin' river,
    Dearer now dan ever.

GLOSSARY

A

A : I. Pronounced short.
a : it ; *e.g.*, " a be'n ondly "= it was only.
a : intrusive word ; *e.g.*, " a t'row "= throw.
a : by ; *e.g.*, " a day "= by day.
a : to,—as in " a school."
a : is ; *e.g.*, " Dis a fe me luck "= This is my luck.
a' : at.
abouten : about.
a come : is coming.
agains' : against.
a-how : how.
aldough : although.
a-limber : gently waving.
an' : and.
'an : than.
anedder : another.
a no : it is not ; *e.g.*, " a no true "= it is not true.
aroun' : around.
as much wort' while : of as much value.
a whe' mumma deh ?—where is mamma ?

B

ball-pan man : vendor of patties.
ban' : band.
bare-face : impudence.

81   F

barn : born. "From A barn "= since I was born ; in all my life.

bat' : bath.

bate : rest.

'batin' : abating.

batter : toil and moil.

beas' : beast ; *i.e.*, horse, mule, or donkey.

beat de eight : do eight hours beat-duty.

becausen : because.

bedouten : without.

behin' : behind.

be'n : was, were ; *e.g.*, " be'n deh fret "= were fretting.

bex' : vexed.

big-tree. A certain big tree in Kingston is the resort of idlers and vicious characters.

bluff : big.

bluff : insult.

boun' : bound ; bind, oblige ; are bound.

'bout, 'bouten : about.

brukfus' : breakfast,—the midday meal.

bud : bird.

bulldog boots : rope-soled slippers.

bumming : cadging, begging for gifts. The *u* has the value of the *oo* in *book*.

bungo : black African.

C

caan' : can't. A *y* is often slipped in after the *c*. Pronounce *kahn* or *kyahn*.

car' : carry.

'causen : because.

'cep' : except.

chat, all deh : all are saying (how bad the policemen are).

chicaney : tricky.

Chiny: the Chinaman.

chock up: right up.

chune dem: tunes.

clot': cloth.

comes-up: familiarity.

constab: policeman; of or belonging to the constabulary. Pronounce the *con* as in *condor*.

corpy: corporal.

'cos: because.

cotch: stand still or lie, and refuse to move. Cotch donkey = a cotching donkey. "Him always cotch" = he always cotches.

couldan: could.

couldn': couldn't.

'counten o': on account of.

couple: few.

cram': crammed.

'cratch: scratch.

cut: sore.

cutliss: cutlass.

D

da': that.

dah: auxiliary; *e.g.*, "dah dun" = is dunning; "dah sabe" = are saving.

dan: than.

dat: that.

de: the.

dead 'way: die away.

deat'; death. "To deat'" = exceedingly.

degra': degrade.

deh: there.

deh: auxiliary; *e.g.*, "me deh go" = I am going; "me deh tell" = I am telling = I tell.

deir: their.

dem: as sign of plural, tacked closely to the preceding word. Thus "man dem" = men; "beas' dem" = beasts.

dem: them, their, they. "All dem boys, etc." = All them (those) boys with eboe-lights (eboe-light sticks), they are waiting there for me.

den: then.

dere: there.

dey: they; "dey do" = they have; "dey'd come" = they had come = they came.

diffran': different.

dih-ya: lengthened form of *dere* (there).

dis: this.

dis: just.

dis ya: this here,—for *this*.

doana: do not.

dog-driver: nickname for a policeman.

do'n: down. The vowel has a short dumb sound, and is followed by a slight *g*.

don'-ca': don't care; inattentive.

don'-ca': nonchalance; indifference.

dough: though.

'dout, 'douten: without.

drop: atom; scrap.

ducky hen: a small short-legged variety of hen.

dus': dust.

dutty: dirty.

dyin' out: very sick.

E

eber: ever.

ebery: every.

eboe-light dem: sticks made of eboe-light or torch-wood.

ef: if.

ef she gwin' go lef' we: if she is going to (go and) leave us.

Ef you 'low, etc.: If you allow the sun to get hot, grass-lice
(small ticks) will surely "make you know" (punish
you).

en': end.

equip': equipped.

F

fabour say: it seems.

fait'ful: faithful.

fat: good food.

favour know: seem to know.

fe: for.

fe: to (sign of the infinitive).

fe go mek: to make.

fe late: to be late.

fe me: my; literally, "for me."

fe you: your, yours.

fingle up: finger; caress.

Finzi: rum.

flockin': crowding round.

'fo': before.

form: pretend, sham.

fortnight: pay-day, which comes once a fortnight.

'fraid: afraid.

frien': friend; in a special sense,—paramour.

full: fill.

fus': first.

fyahn: fern.

G

ge'man: gentleman; gentleman's.

get fe write: get the opportunity of writing.

gie'm: give him; gave him.

gill: three farthings. "Gill bread"=loaf costing three farthings.

good, 'Fo we tu'n: hardly had we turned when......

go'p: go up.

grass-lice: small ticks.

gro'l: growl.

groun': ground.

grudge: envy.

gwin': going (to).

gwin' go lef' we: going to (go and) leave us.

H

hab: have.

hamper: panniers.

han': hand.

harse: horse.

hea': hear.

him: his: *e.g.*, him nose=his nose.

h'is'in': hoisting. Pronounce with long *i*.

hol' up: hold up,—*i.e.*, neglect to pay.

hound: chase.

hu't: hurt, hurts.

I

i': it.

in-a: into the; in the; in.

ingredients: salt, pepper, butter, &c.

J

jack : donkey
jes' : just.
jesmy : jasmine.   The buds are put in with the letter.
jine : join.
John-to-whit : the red-eyed greenlet.   The name is imita-
     tive of the bird's note.
Judge de feelin's : Judge the feelings=just think.
juice : deuce.

K

ketch : catch.
kep' : be kept.
'kin : skin.
kin' : kind.   Pronounce with long *i*.
kit : job.
know, mek you : equivalent to the slang phrase "give you
     beans."
ko : look.
kue : hi !

L

laka dis : like this.   The *lak* has the value of French *lac*.
Lard : Lord.
larn : learn, teach.
last, fe de : for the last time.
lay : lies ; lie.
leas' : least.
ledder : ladder.
lee : little.
lef' : left ; leave.

lib : live.
li'l, lilly : little.
limber : see *a-limber*.
'lone : alone.
'long : along.
love' : loved.
lub : love.

M

mac : shilling, shillings ; short for *macaroni*.
manchinic : Martinique bananas.
marnin', soon a : early in the morning.
me : my.　It is written thus in order to remind the reader
　　　that the *y* of *my* is almost invariably short.
me no know : I don't know.
me poor boy : I, poor fellow that I am ; poor I.
mek : make ; let.
mek we : let us.
mek you know : see *know*.
mell' : meddle.
'member : remember.
mese'f : myself.
middle.　" In de middle road "=in the middle of the road.
mighta : might.
min' : mind.　Pronounce the *i* long.
mo' : more.
mountain-side : in the mountains.
mout' : mouth.
mudder : mother.
mus'n' : must not.
mus' smart : must be smart.
mussy : mercy.
mus' wukin' overdue : must be working overtime.

N

'neat' : beneath.

neber trus', &c. : never trust theirs as I can mine.

neider : neither.

no fe her own han' ?=is it not her own hand ?

no lef' me : do not leave me.

nong : now.   The vowel sound is very dumb and short.

northers : north winds.

not'in' : nothing.   Pronounce *nuttin'*.

'nough, 'nuff : enough.

no wuk : don't work.

nummo : no more.

nyam : eat.   A monosyllable like *yam*.

O

ob : of.

ober-bex' : over-vexed.

ole : old.

ole-time : of or belonging to former times.

'ole : whole.

ondly : only.

ord'ly : orderly.

out : out of.

owna : own.

P

'panish-needle grass : Spanish Needle,—a fodder plant.

partly : nearly.

pas' : past.

pass : path.

petater : potato.
play : pretend.
play out : deceive.
plenty : many.
'pon : upon.
poo' : poor.
'port : report.
pupperlicks : head over heels ; turning somersaults.

Q

'queeze : squeeze.

R

rag : (such) fine.
raise : contribution.
rash : rations.
rather tryin' : trying our best.
res' : rest.
'res' : arrest.
ring grand, was : rang out grandly.
risky : flirty.
roun' : round.
roun-a : round the.
rule : regulations ; discipline.
rum's up : rum being about.

S

sabe : save.
Sah : Sir.
sake o' : on account of.

sal' : salt.

sall, in them : having a fine time of it. Pronounce *sahl.*

say. This is often an intrusive word of no significance:
e.g., " Jes' becausen say dem poor so "=Just
because they are so poor.

Say mumma, &c.?=Does he say mamma is sinking ?

see'm : see him.

seems : it seems.

self : even. " No wut gill self "=not even worth a gill.

sen' : send.

sence : since.

se'p me king : so help me God.

shedah : shadow.

shet : shut.

'side : beside.

shouldn' : shouldn't.

slimber : slender.

S.M.: Sergeant Major.

snappy : ill-tempered.

so : such.

so-so : only ; nothing but ; bare.

soun' : sound.

sport : sporting character.

'spose : I suppose.

stan' : stand.

swea' : swear.

sweet me : give me pleasure.

Syrian-boy : negro working for a Syrian pedlar.

T

talk, wi' sure : my eboe-light will surely talk,—*i.e.,* teach
you a lesson by means of the drubbing it will give
you.

'tall : at all.

'tan' deh hide : stand there and hide.

tarra : the other.   Vowel-sound as in *t'other*.

tatters all : all tattered.

te-day : to-day,—usually accented on the first syllable.

tek : take.

tell : till.

'ten' : attend.

tendin' : looking after.

t'enk : thank.

'teppin' : stepping.

'ter : after.

them : their.

ti' : till.

t'ick : thick.

tief : thieve, steal.

t'ing : thing.

t'ink : think.

'tion' : attention (standing to).

togeder : together.

told good-night : wished good-night.

to'n : town.   The vowel is very dumb.

'top : stop.

'top sleep : stop sleeping.

t'ought : thought.

'traight : straight.

trick : tricky.

'trong : strong.

t'rough : through.

t'row : throw.

trus' : trust; give on trust; take on trust.

try, wid all de etc. : try as hard as she may.

tu'n : turn.   Pronounce *tu'nin'* tunnin.

tup : twopence of the old Jamaica coinage ; three halfpence
      of the new.

two-an'-four : the ordinary policeman's daily pay.

U

udder : other, other's.

unno : you. The *u* sounds between *o* and *u*, and the final
    o is more like *oo*, but very short.

use' : used.

ushal : usual (with the middle syllable unpronounced).
    Except for this omission, the pronunciation is
    identical.

V

v'ice : voice. " Ha' no v'ice "=can't say anything.

W

wan' : want. The *to* after *want* is generally omitted. Thus
    " wan' go "=want to go ; " want see "=want to see.

warra : what. The value of the *a* is unchanged.

way : away.

we : us ; our.

weader : weather.

wha' : what. " Wha' de doctor t'ink ? "=What does the
    doctor think ? " Wha' de use ? "=What is the
    use ?—Pronounce the *a* precisely as in *what*.

wha' it : what.

whe' : where.

whe' : who, whom. The *e* is short, as in *wet*.

wi' : will ; will be.

wi' : with.

wid : with.

won' : won't.

wort' while, wut while : worth while,—meaning profitable, serviceable, useful.

wouldan : would,—not to be confused with the following.

wouldn' : would not.

wud : word.

wuk : work.

wul' : world.

wut, no : not worth ; is no use.

wutless, wutlessness : worthlessness, badness, rascality.

wutten price : worth his price.

wut while : worth while, *i.e.*, of any use and profit.

Y

ya : here.

yah : do you hear ?—often thrown in without any particular meaning.

yerry-yerries : minnows.

yet : hereafter ; in time to come.

you' : your. The *ou* pronounced as in *you*.

you sick : you are sick.

ISBN 0-8369-8982-1

9 780836 989823